WHY
HONOR
MATTERS

WHY HONOR MATTERS

Tamler Sommers

BASIC BOOKS

New York

Basic Books
Hachette Book Group
1290 Avenue of the Americas, New York, NY 10104
www.basicbooks.com

Printed in the United States of America

First Edition: May 2018

Published by Basic Books, an imprint of Perseus Books, LLC, a subsidiary of Hachette Book Group, Inc. The Basic Books name and logo is a trademark of the Hachette Book Group.

The publisher is not responsible for websites (or their content) that are not owned by the publisher.

Library of Congress Cataloging-in-Publication Data
Names: Sommers, Tamler, 1970-author.
Title: Why honor matters / Tamler Sommers.
Description: First Edition. | New York, N.Y. : Basic Books, an imprint of
    Perseus Books, LLC, a subsidiary of Hachette Book Group, Inc., 2018. |
    Includes bibliographical references and index.
Identifiers: LCCN 2018001837| ISBN 9780465098873 (hardcover) |
    ISBN9780465098880 (ebook)
Subjects: LCSH: Honor.
Classification: LCC BJ1533.H8 S63 2018 | DDC 179/.9—dc23
LC record available at https://lccn.loc.gov/2018001837

Print book interior design by Jouve.

ISBNs: 978-0-465-09887-3 (hardcover); 978-0-465-09888-0 (ebook)

LSC-C

10 9 8 7 6 5 4 3 2 1

To Jen and Eliza
and to the memory of my parents,
Fred Sommers and Shula Sommers

CONTENTS

HONOR MATTERS

Who's your favorite character in *The Godfather?* Ask that question to ten people, and I'll bet you the cost of this book that at least five answer "Sonny." Everyone loves Sonny: Santino Corleone, played by James Caan, the hothead, the oldest of the don's three sons, the one who gets gunned down at the tollbooth about halfway through the movie. But why does everyone love him? Think about it for a second. He's violent and impulsive, he cheats on his wife regularly, and he was a terrible interim don after his father was shot. He starts a war with the family he thinks is responsible, which is bad for business and unites the other Mafia families against him. Even worse, the attempt on his father's life was Sonny's fault to begin with. Before he's taken out at the tollbooth, Sonny almost leads the Corleone family to ruin. But we love him anyway. Why?

Here's why: we love him for his passion, courage, guts, integrity, and most of all his loyalty to his family. When Sonny learns that Connie, his sister, has been abused by her husband, Carlo, Sonny doesn't hesitate for a second: he heads straight for the corner to find Carlo and gives him the beating that every filmgoer knows he deserves. When it comes to defending his family, Sonny doesn't calculate the best move, the most profitable move—Michael is the calculating member of the family. Sonny just acts out of stubborn passion and a sense of honor. Repeatedly in the film we hear characters say "It's only business." Not Sonny, though. It's never "only business" for Sonny. That's what gets him killed at the tollbooth: his uncompromising and unprofitable loyalty—to his sister, his father—and his honor.

Our attitudes toward Sonny reflect a more general ambivalence about honor in the modern West. Indeed, *ambivalence* may be too weak a word. When it comes to honor, we're positively schizophrenic. On the one hand, we have deep nostalgia for the honorable way of life. Whole genres of literature and film feed off this nostalgia. Not just mob movies, but westerns, film noir, revenge stories, Jane Austen novels, even musicals (think *Hamilton*). The virtues associated with honor such as courage, loyalty, solidarity, accountability, and integrity are precisely what we find lacking in the modern world. But at the same time, we find many aspects of honor to be absurd, petty, and morally reprehensible. After all, doesn't honor lead to blood feuds, pointless duels, vigilantism, revenge, racism, nationalism, terrorism, bullying, and violence against women? Isn't one of the signs of civilization's progress that we've put honor in the rearview mirror and replaced it with a commitment to dignity, equality, and human rights?

Most contemporary Western thinkers certainly seem to think so. Steven Pinker, for example, in his celebrated book *The Better*

Angels of Our Nature attributed much of the decline of violence in the world to secular humanist values that have swept aside "fetishisized virtues such as…honor, heroism, and glory." To critics like Pinker, these honor-related virtues are primitive and dispensable, like our early beliefs about the solar system, worth studying only to see how we went wrong. Another psychologist, Ryan Brown, refers to honor as a disease, a syndrome that must be eradicated from the American psyche. Meanwhile, with very few exceptions, moral philosophers have ignored honor as a topic of serious study. Honor is hardly mentioned in the contemporary ethical literature. It's too messy, irrational, backward, and weird. It doesn't fit comfortably within the Western liberal rule-based ethical tradition that has dominated moral philosophy since the Enlightenment. Philosophers don't feel the need to criticize honor, because it isn't taken seriously in the first place. It's just off the table, "exiled to some philosophical St. Helena," as Anthony Appiah puts it, "left to contemplate its wilting epaulets and watch its once gleaming sword corrode in the salt air."

Some have gone so far as to question honor's very reality. Pinker calls it a "strange commodity that exists because everyone believes that everyone else believes that it exists." And such doubts have been with us for ages. Falstaff, for example, in a famous speech from Shakespeare's *Henry IV, Part I*, asks:

> Can honour set-to a leg? No. Or an arm? No. Or take away the grief of a wound? No. Honour hath no skill in surgery, then? No. What is honour? A word. What is in that word "honour"? What

is that "honour"? Air. A trim reckoning! Who hath it? He that
died o' Wednesday. Doth he feel it? No. Doth he hear it? No.
'Tis insensible then? Yea, to the dead. But will it not live with the
living? No. Why? Detraction will not suffer it. Therefore I'll none
of it. Honour is a mere scutcheon.

To Falstaff, honor is just a word, a "scutcheon," not a tangible thing
with real value. We still often speak of honor this way, as a shared
hallucination, a pyramid scheme propped up by false notions and
petty drives for prestige.

Part of the problem, especially for philosophers, is that honor
is so hard to pin down. Philosophers like their concepts crisp and
definable. The dominant approach in philosophy is called concep-
tual analysis: an attempt to come up with necessary and sufficient
conditions that capture every instance that the concept is used.
Honor emphatically resists this kind of approach. I've been writing
this book on honor for three years, and I'm still hard-pressed to give
a concise description of what it is. Think of how many categories
we associate with the concept: honor cultures, honor systems, honor
codes, honor values, medals of honor, honorary degrees, honor rolls,
honor groups, honor societies, honor worlds. Honor can be a verb
("Honor thy mother and father"), a noun ("We must preserve the
family honor," "I graduated with honors"), an adjective (honor society), and a form of address ("Your honor, I object!"). In contrast
to the dominant ethical theories with their small set of universal principles, honor spins a dizzying web of values, virtues, codes,
commandments, and prohibitions that are constantly changing and

evolving. And honor makes no pretense to universality. The honor of the Mafia is different from the honor of hockey teams, which is different from the honor of an Eskimo tribe. Anyone who wants to define honor with even a hint of precision is in for a rude surprise. (Believe me, I know.)

But "undefinable" isn't the same as "unreal." Over the past ten years, I've come to believe that honor is both real and valuable— indispensable, even, for living a good life in a good and just society. I'm convinced that our collective rejection of honor has come at great cost and that reclaiming it can improve our lives and our society. This book is my attempt to explain why.

Why Me? Why Honor?

I'm no stranger myself to ambivalence about honor. At the start of my career, I was on the side of the critics and the dismissers. I promoted a more rational approach to ethics—and especially to my area of expertise: blame, praise, and responsibility. Yet part of me always rebelled against what I was putting down on paper, in my articles. There was always a nagging voice in the back of my mind: "You don't believe what you're writing here."

But let me back up. As I say, nobody teaches you about honor in academic philosophy. Like most philosophers, I was trained in the Western ethical tradition, which meant that I spent my time engaging in debates between harm-based theories (such as utilitarianism) and dignity- or rights-based theories (from Locke, Kant, and John Rawls). It was during the writing of my book on free will and moral responsibility that I stumbled upon research of so-called honor cultures, societies where honor was a central part of their value system. To my surprise, these cultures had a starkly different way of understanding responsibility and its connection to freedom. Like most philosophers in my area, I was obsessed with questions about how we can be truly free in a world governed by the laws of nature. How can we blame, praise, and punish people for actions that didn't originate in them but were caused by factors that might trace back all the way to the big bang? Honor cultures didn't struggle with this problem, because they didn't think a strong form of free will was necessary for holding people responsible for their actions. They didn't regard the absence of control as an excuse for behavior. In honor cultures, you can get blamed for actions that weren't intentional, for actions committed by relatives, ancestors, or other members of your group.

My first reaction was a common one for Westerners. How interesting! How quaint! These odd and primitive people haven't truly understood the deep problems of free will and determinism. But the more research I did on cultural differences, the clearer it became that we were the weird ones, not them. Most societies throughout history and even today are on the side of the honor cultures. The exceptions were those of us who live in WEIRD (Western, educated, industrialized, rich, and democratic) societies. Okay, I thought, but maybe we were just more rational about freedom and its relation to moral responsibility. Again, further investigation convinced me this was not the case. The alternate perspectives were often coherent and empirically sound—in short, just as rational as our own practices on responsibility, blame, and praise. And that became the central thesis of my book.

But my interest in honor didn't stop there. The more research I did on honor cultures of all sorts, the more I found myself drawn to various aspects of their way of life. The strong norms of hospitality, for example. The social cohesion and solidarity, where selfish interests take a backseat to the interests of the group. The emphasis on courage, integrity, and accountability—in honor cultures, you have to demonstrate that you're willing to stand up for yourself and your principles even in the face of risks to your safety and material interests. Which leads to plenty of excitement and drama. Not the overwrought social media drama I had become accustomed to, but real drama—where the deepest part of your identity is at stake. And finally, people in honor cultures seem to have a strong sense of purpose and meaning—there's less existential angst, and the people know what they're living for, what's important, and why.

Courage, integrity, solidarity, drama, hospitality, a sense of purpose and meaning—these are attractive values and characteristics, important for living a good and worthwhile life. But there was something else drawing me to honor too, something more fundamental and harder to describe. Though I subscribe to liberal values of toleration and respect for individual freedom, I've come to believe that the Western liberal approach to ethics is deeply misguided. The approach is too systematic, too idealized and abstract—incapable of reckoning with the messy complexity of the real world. The most influential moral philosophers of the last several hundred years—Immanuel Kant, John Stuart Mill, and John Rawls—derived their theories from a small set of allegedly self-evident principles. They try to show what an ideal society of rational agents would look like. The elegance and simplicity of their theories mislead us into thinking that their principles, properly applied, will result in a perfectly just society. If we just execute the game plan properly, in other words, our problems will be solved. But no simple theory can capture something as chaotic and contradictory as human nature or human society. The more abstract and simple the theory, the less it can tell us about our actual lives and struggles.

Idealized, systematic, abstract, and universalizable—honor has none of these attributes. Honor, unlike dignity, is not abstract; it's grounded in fact. Honor is real only when people recognize and acknowledge it. Honor codes are local, not universal, tailored to the particular needs of each community. Most important, honor codes are tailored to people as they are, not how we wish them to be or how we imagine they would be if they were "rational." Honor is full of compromises; it deals in grays rather than black and white. It seeks better alternatives, not ideal alternatives. In short, honor is a thoroughly nonideal form of value, which allows it to operate with a more accurate understanding of human psychology.

Throughout the book I'll try to convince you that these two aspects of honor—its attractive virtues and the unsystematic nature of its codes—are intimately connected. Honor frameworks recognize that it's not easy to be virtuous: to take risks and act with integrity and solidarity. We need motivation, what evolutionary biologists and behavioral economists have called "commitment devices," to overcome our natural impulse toward comfort and safety. Honor frameworks offer a rich tapestry of codes and incentives to counteract this impulse. They have rituals and traditions for bringing people together, for celebrating exceptional people and behavior, and for holding people accountable. Codes that adapt to human strengths and weaknesses can be effective tools for motivation. These motivational tools are absent in the ethics of Western liberalism because of its idealized nature.

The central thesis of this book, then, is that honor has a lot to teach us and that we are wrong to ignore or reject it. It's undeniable that our commitment to Enlightenment values has brought tremendous benefits for individual freedom and respect for human rights. At its best, it produces a society with more equal treatment, one that respects its citizens and allows them to pursue their interests and goals without interference. But liberal Enlightenment morality is not perfect, and it's not sufficient. It can also lead to increasing alienation, selfish individualism, and a high-minded disregard for the struggles and suffering of others. Now don't worry—this isn't going to be a cranky "modern society is going to hell" *Slouching Towards Gomorrah* kind of book. I like my Netflix, Subaru, and SodaStream as much as anyone. But the comforts and safety of modern life shouldn't blind us to its terrible problems. Reclaiming honor as a core value can help us address these problems, and this book will show us how.

And Yet…

I know how tempting it can be to romanticize honor—I led off with an example from *The Godfather*, for God's sake. It's easy to romanticize something that provides excitement, drama, and great stories. I'm an academic—as the Kissinger quote goes, our conflicts are so bitter because the stakes are so small. At times I worry that I'm what you might call an "honor tourist"—someone who takes in the sights of honor in books and movies, who can enjoy the grandeur without having to endure the costs of living there on a daily basis. And to be sure, honor has its share of heavy costs, a well-known dark side. There's a reason that Westerners have turned away from it. I showed an early draft of this book to a friend, and she was wary. Trump had just been elected; the "alt-right" was gaining steam. Groups that feel humiliated by external forces or a larger governing society often turn to honor rhetoric to organize and motivate their movement. And what about all that morally atrocious baggage, my friend asked me: What about honor's connection to tribalism, violence, and misogyny? What about the blood feuds, the duels, the aggression? Honor can trap people in rigid social roles, limiting their freedom to determine their own identity and conception of a good life. In many honor cultures, women especially seem to bear the brunt of these restrictions. Honor has no essential commitment to a notion of universal human rights, so its codes can, and have, sanctioned morally odious behavior on a significant scale. Any honest reckoning of honor must take these concerns very seriously.

So while I plan to offer a defense of honor, it is not a defense of *unconstrained* honor. If you've picked up this book looking for a subtle or sideways defense of racism or sexism, you're going to be disappointed. My conclusion will be that honor systems flourish only when they're effectively contained. Fortunately, honor can be contained; we can restore honor into a larger value system while at the same time limiting its potential abuses. As we'll see, many communities and institutions are doing this already, and there is potential for many more. We can fruitfully apply basic principles of honor to some of our most challenging problems: risk aversion, alienation, education, policing, and mass incarceration. And we can do all of this without taking our eyes off the dangers that my friend worries about.

The Plan and a Plea

So here's the plan. In Chapter One, I'll do my best to explain what honor is and how it functions, contrasting it with the ethical concept that has come to replace it in many minds—dignity. In Chapter Two, I'll examine some of the consequences of abandoning honor in the modern West. The next three chapters explore an aspect of honor-related values. They aim to illuminate both the strengths and the weaknesses of honor codes in relation to community (Chapter Three), violence (Chapter Four), and revenge (Chapter Five). Chapter Six is the most ambitious and, in my mind, the most important chapter in the book. It begins with a critique of the Western approach to criminal justice and finds a direct connection between its tragic defects and the rationalistic dignity-based morality at its core. I then describe an exciting new movement in criminal punishment called "restorative justice" that offers enormous moral benefits, but requires us to reorient our philosophical understanding of punishment. I show how restorative justice applies the basic values of honor to criminal conflicts—with impressive results. It is a prime example of the contained form of honor that I wish to defend. Finally, in Chapter Seven, I offer a more general model of what contained honor looks like and how we can implement it to our advantage.

Now for the plea. As I said earlier, honor is full of compromises; it is a nonideal form of value. To borrow a metaphor from philosopher Otto Neurath, honor is continuously building and repairing a boat that is already out at sea. Consequently, honor's critics can always come up with hypothetical cases of injustice that honor cannot solve *even in principle*. So my plea is simple. As you evaluate my argument, resist that urge to come up with abstract hypothetical objections. Compare my examples of honor systems with actual alternatives, not idealized alternatives. Here's an analogy (one that hits a little too close to home for me). Imagine living in a house that badly needs repair. As you compare the contractors, you should choose the one who can actually make the house better, not the one who can best imagine the blueprint of a perfect house. The same thinking applies to improving society.

A final word before I begin. I have no political ax to grind, and this book has no political agenda, though I'm sure some will take it that way. For what it's worth, I tend to be a liberal on most issues—though not as far to the left as some of my academic colleagues. I've made no effort to hide my political opinions, but for the most part my defense of honor is entirely independent of them. And that's a good thing too—because the politics of honor are all over the place. Some honor values are quite progressive: egalitarianism, anti-individualism, striving for the common good. (Hillary

Clinton's "It takes a village" would be an accurate motto for many honor cultures.) Indeed, the rejection of abstract theorizing and the emphasis on personal connections and feelings are in line with some aspects of feminist philosophy and their critique of theorists like John Rawls. Other honor values have more conservative (and less feminist) associations: agonism, tribal loyalty, concern for female purity. In matters of policy, my examples of contained honor—such as restorative justice, police reform, hip-hop culture—probably find greater support among liberals than conservatives. On the other hand, the core commitments of honor cultures may be more in line with traditional conservatism: a mistrust of centralized power and the emphasis on the local and the personal over the universal and the impartial.

Whatever your impression about the politics of honor, try not to let it affect how you evaluate my argument. The stakes are too high for that. Our collective rejection of honor has come at a great cost to modern life. The downside to honor is real, but it can be contained rather than dismissed. By the end of this book, I hope to convince you that reclaiming honor can help us lead better and more fulfilling lives as individuals and as a society.

But first I need to explain what it is that I'm defending. And that is no simple task.

CHAPTER 1

CONTOURS OF HONOR

Taking Care of Business

Sean Tracey, a young relief pitcher for the Chicago White Sox, had appeared in only two Major League Baseball games when he was ordered to hit Texas third baseman Hank Blalock. The order came from his manager, Ozzie Guillén—retaliation for one of his own players getting beaned earlier in the game. Tracey didn't have great control of pitches, and he was nervous. His first attempt came close to Blalock's chin but missed him. He then threw the next pitch outside to avoid suspicion. He threw at Blalock again on the third pitch, but again he missed. Then came the decision that would alter Tracey's career: he tried to get Blalock out, figuring it would at least give his team the best chance to win the game. And Blalock obliged, grounding to third for an easy out. Immediately, a furious Guillén stormed to the mound and yanked Tracey from the game, yelling at him all the way to the dugout. Guillén continued berating Tracey in the dugout, in front of both his teammates and a television audience.

With nowhere to hide, Tracey sat on the bench and pulled his jersey up over his head, "doing his best to disappear in plain sight." And before long he did disappear—from the White Sox anyway. Tracey was sent down to the Minors two days later and then released by the organization in the off-season. Blalock was the last hitter Tracey faced as a member of the Chicago White Sox.

What did Tracey do wrong? Why was he berated for doing what pitchers are supposed to do—get batters out? Tracey had violated baseball's honor code. He hadn't retaliated; he hadn't evened the score: he didn't defend his teammates. As previous White Sox manager Charlie Manuel put it, "We will not tolerate the guys who are the heart and soul of this team getting hit…. That's part of the 'fearless' package and the 'respect' package. We're not looking to start anything, but we're definitely not looking to back off anything either."

Beanball feuds have been part of baseball since the beginning. As I write this, my beloved Red Sox are in a bitter one with the Baltimore Orioles that has lasted for weeks and resulted in multiple suspensions. Outsiders are fond of ridiculing baseball's dizzying array of unwritten honor codes and rules: Don't jog around the bases too slowly after a home run. If you do, you'll get hit. Don't try to steal a base in a blowout. If you do, you'll get hit. Don't try to bunt your way on to first base when the pitcher is throwing a no-hitter. If you do…You get the idea. Virtually all of baseball's unwritten codes revolve around the notion of respect: respect for the game, for your teammates, and for other teams. When players suspect they're being shown up or disrespected, that's when the fireworks begin.

When they're not making fun of these rules, baseball journalists like to moralize against them—the vendettas, the vigilante justice especially. And that's not surprising—most journalists operate within the moral framework of dignity, and honor and dignity understand conflicts in very different terms. In a dignity framework, all offenses should be addressed by an impartial third party—the league office, in this case. In honor cultures, turning to third parties when you've been insulted or offended indicates weakness or cowardice and a lack of self-respect. In honor cultures, people are expected to handle their own business.

My goal in this chapter is to map out the contours of honor and illustrate the ways it differs from other moral concepts and frameworks, such as dignity. A clearer sense of what honor is all about will help us see whether it is worth preserving.

Honor Groups

Honor is social; it cannot exist for individuals in isolation. For honor frameworks to function, they need what I'll refer to as an honor group—a collection of people bound by a set of principles and values. Honor groups vary in size and structure. Their boundaries can be well defined (navy SEALs, Mafia families, hockey teams) or loosely defined (American southerners, chefs, stand-up comics). Each honor group has a set of codes, formal and informal, that determines how honor and dishonor are distributed among its members.

Anthropologist Frank Stewart introduced a helpful distinction between two dimensions of honor. The first is "horizontal." Having horizontal honor means that you're entitled to a level of respect just by virtue of belonging to the honor group. If you're a "made man" in the Sicilian Mafia, for example, you're entitled to an assortment of privileges within the Mafia structure. People in the community must treat you with respect and deference. You have distinctive forms of address ("a friend of ours"), you rarely pay for drinks or dinners, and other mafiosi can't steal from you, assault you, or hit on your wife or girlfriends. A defining feature of horizontal honor is that it's distributed equally to all group members. Another is that it is not tied to a specific action or achievement. We say "your honor" to judges simply because they are judges, not because of any verdict or decision they may have written. Unless they step down or get disbarred, they are entitled to this form of respect. We allow uniformed military to board planes early and often say "Thank you for your service" without having any idea what he or she did to serve the country. Eighteenth-century British aristocrats could move in the best social circles even if they had no specific accomplishments under their belt. Having horizontal honor is like being a member of a club. And membership has its privileges.

Membership also has its obligations and responsibilities. Made men must pay tribute to the Mafia family and risk life and limb when called upon to defend it. They are bound by the omertà vow of silence that prohibits cooperation with outside authorities—even when the price of silence is a long prison term. Soldiers are bound to follow orders from their commanding officers and never to desert their unit. Captains must go down with the ship. Failure to live up to your responsibilities can strip you of horizontal honor. As

Stewart observes, horizontal honor is easier to lose than to acquire. Just ask Sean Tracey.

Indeed, for some people, horizontal honor can be impossible to acquire. Commoners in Victorian England couldn't crack the aristocracy no matter how witty or talented they were. Jimmy Conway and Henry Hill from *Goodfellas* (played by Robert De Niro and Ray Liotta, respectively) could never be made men because they weren't pure Italians. But not all honor groups have such impregnable barriers for entry. In principle, anyone can become a naval officer, a judge, a hockey player, or a comedian. But it can't be easy either. Honor groups must be exclusive if they wish to preserve the prestige and status that come from belonging to them.

Honor groups typically take great pride in their exclusivity; they publicize it and use it to motivate the people in the group to perform exceptional acts. Perhaps the most famous example is King Henry's Saint Crispin's Day speech to his troops in *Henry V*:

> *From this day to the ending of the world,*
> *But we in it shall be remembered—*
> *We few, we happy few, we band of brothers;*
> *For he to-day that sheds his blood with me*
> *Shall be my brother; be he ne'er so vile,*
> *This day shall gentle his condition;*
> *And gentlemen in England now a-bed*
> *Shall think themselves accurs'd they were not here,*
> *And hold their manhoods cheap whiles any speaks*
> *That fought with us upon Saint Crispin's day.*

In the speech King Henry employs the idea of horizontal honor to inspire men to risk their lives in battle. He doesn't deny that the English gentlemen "now a-bed" had a much better chance of living to see tomorrow. Instead, he appeals to his soldiers' sense of pride of belonging to the happy few, the band of brothers. The more exclusive the group, the more people want to belong to it and the more incentive group members have for living up to their responsibilities. This psychological insight is no less relevant in our own day: elite military groups around the world employ similar rhetoric. The slogan "The Few, the Proud, the Marines" is so effective that it appears on the Madison Avenue Advertising Walk of Fame.

The other dimension of honor in Stewart's account is "vertical." Once they belong to an honor group, members compete for vertical honor to improve their status within the group's hierarchy. In contrast to horizontal honor, vertical honor is acquired through one's actions and achievements and cannot, by definition, be distributed equally among the group members. The honor culture of ancient Greece had three different words to distinguish three categories of vertical honor. The first, *geras*, or *gera* for the plural, refers to the more material, tangible forms of honor. After a successful raid, for example, the kings would divvy up the bounty (jewels, armor, captured slaves, and mistresses) in accordance with how much each warrior had contributed to the victory. The more value you had to the group, the more *gera* you would receive. *Geras* therefore has both material and symbolic value. It can add to your material wealth, but more important your *gera* serves as an indication of your worthiness. Some modern examples of *gera* include medals, titles, salary raises, named chairs, the Heisman Trophy, Academy Awards, or the Nobel Prize. Meryl Streep's three Oscars along with her twenty nominations may not be worth much money (for someone in her income bracket anyway), but they serve to mark her as the greatest film actress of her generation.

Not surprisingly, the distribution of *gera* is something that people in honor cultures take very personally. When Agamemnon takes away Achilles's slave mistress, Briseis, whom he had acquired as *geras* from a previous battle, Achilles is so enraged that he stops fighting for the Greeks in the Trojan War. The source of Achilles's rage isn't his attachment to Briseis, but rather the symbolic challenge to his honor. By stripping Achilles of his *geras*, Agamemnon sends the signal "You're not as valuable as you think you are to the Greek army." Achilles can't let this stand, and he decides to prove his worth by sitting out the war, knowing it will lead to massive casualties for the Greeks until he returns.

The second Greek word for vertical honor, *tîmê*, refers to a more intangible form of honor. Your *tîmê* represents your worth, your value, to the group. (Your *geras* can be a marker for your *tîmê*.) Although *tîmê* is intangible, it does have tangible effects. Your *tîmê* determines how people treat you relative to others—as an object of admiration and deference or one of ridicule and contempt. And it influences how you regard yourself—with pride or shame. If you live in an honor culture, your *tîmê* is a significant part of your identity, what constitutes you as a person. Anthropologist Julian Pitt-Rivers describes this form of honor as "the value of a person in his own eyes but also in the eyes of society." *Tîmê* has both public and objective criteria. You can't have *tîmê* unless you're truly valuable to the group. But your objective value isn't sufficient for *tîmê*; your group must acknowledge your worthiness as well. William Ian Miller, an expert on the honor cultures of the Icelandic Sagas, captures this idea well in his book *Humiliation*:

> In an honor based culture there was no self-respect independent of the respect of others, no private sense of "hey, I'm quite something" unless it was confirmed publicly. Honor was then not just a matter of the individual; it necessarily involved a group, and the group included all those people worthy of competing with you for honor. Your status in this group was the measure of your honor, and your status was achieved at the expense of the other group members who were not only your competitors for scarce honor but also the arbiters of whether you had it or not.

Of course, everyone—honor culture or no—enjoys being recognized for their accomplishments. Everyone likes to be admired. The difference is one of degree. In honor cultures, public recognition constitutes a central part of one's self-worth. That said, it's a common misconception to think that public recognition is the *only* thing that matters in honor cultures. It's just as important to be worthy of your acknowledged honor, to prove to yourself and the community that you've earned your *tîmê*.

Another misconception about honor is that it's always zero-sum, gained at the expense of the others. This is often true but not always. The most respected players on American football teams, for example, earn the title of captain. The title is honorific (so to speak), and it doesn't come with additional salary or benefits—a better parking space, at most. But captains take great pride in the title because it's a sign of how much their teammates value their leadership. Not everyone can be a captain, but there is no set number of captains either. Teams can have more than one captain, or they can have none at all; it all depends on who is worthy of the title. Another example comes from the world of stand-up comedy. Comedians compete to be known as the "comic's comic"—the person who kills not just with drunken audiences but also with a tough crowd of fellow comics. Like "captain," the title that brings no money or even celebrity, comic's comics usually don't appeal to the widest audiences. But it's arguably the highest form of praise within the group of comics. As with "captain," there is no set number of comic's comics. But there can't be too many either. Like all forms of honor, *timê* needs to be a relatively scarce resource to be genuine. The Comedy Cellar in New York is famous for its "comedians table," where comics compete in a battle of vicious insults. Comedian Patrice O'Neal was a legend in the comedy world for his performance at the table. Although he had only one stand-up special under his belt, he was considered a true comic's comic. Every year after his untimely death at the age of forty-one, comics from all over the world perform a benefit to support his family and honor his memory.

The final category of Greek honor is *kleos*, often translated as "glory." *Kleos* is the highest form of honor and the easiest to describe. In the Greek world, if you have *kleos*, the poets will tell your story for generations. They'll compose epics of your adventures and odes to your character and your virtues—your name will ring out forever. The greatest warriors, like Achilles, Hector, Ajax, and Odysseus, and the most virtuous women, like Penelope and Antigone, had *kleos*, which is precisely why we still read about them today. Woody Allen once wrote that he did not want to be immortal through his work; he wanted to be immortal by not dying. *Kleos* doesn't quite give you that, but it gives you all the immortality that it's possible to have.

Examples of people with *kleos* in our own time include Babe Ruth, Rosa Parks, Jackie Robinson, Winston Churchill, Balzac, Tolstoy, Susan B. Anthony, and Abraham Lincoln—the people we studied in school and our children study and their children will study. King Henry appeals to *kleos* when he says that the band of brothers will be remembered "from this day to the ending of the world." When presidents start talking about their historical legacies, they're making their bids for *kleos*. The prospect of *kleos* provides people with incentives to perform actions of bravery and heroism. Political scientist Sharon Krause documents the role of reputation and a sense of honor for motivating heroes like Frederick Douglass, Martin Luther King Jr., and the women suffragettes. (Abraham Lincoln, for example, paused before signing the Emancipation Proclamation to say, "If my name ever goes down in the history books, it will be for this act.")

Whereas honor systems offer plenty of incentives—tangible and otherwise—for maintaining a high reputation, dignity cultures are mildly embarrassed about rewarding good behavior. Dignity embraces the Kantian idea that people should be moral only for the sake of being moral, not for any personal benefit. In real life, however, rewards are more effective for promoting virtuous behavior. Lacking such incentives, cultures of dignity focus more on preventing wrongdoing than promoting virtue. They have elaborate systems of punishment for deterring wrongdoing but no organized way to encourage people to go above and beyond the call of duty. *Kleos* can move people to go well above and beyond the call of duty for the good of the group.

All the forms of honor I've described in this section have motivational power. This robust motivational structure is largely absent in Western liberal morality, and it's perhaps the greatest potential advantage of reclaiming honor as a core value. Liberalism, with its focus on human dignity and individual liberty, gives us plenty of reasons to refrain from wrongdoing—through punishment and other mechanisms—but provides little to inspire exceptional or heroic behavior. Since individual and group honor is so central to self-conception, people in honor groups go to great lengths to increase rather than decrease it. Of course, honor's motivational power is an advantage only if it motivates good behavior. In the last section of this chapter, we'll explore some characteristic norms of behavior in honor cultures. But first let's turn to the source of honor's motivational power: the connection between honor and identity, honor and the self.

Honor, Dignity, and Identity

In a seminal essay, "On the Obsolescence of the Concept of Honor," sociologist Peter Berger argues that the primary distinction between honor and dignity involves their relation to identity. Honor cultures, writes Berger, have a relatively stable set of institutions and institutional roles. The roles adopted by the group members constitute a significant part of their identity, their sense of who they are as people. The modern concept of dignity, by contrast, "implies that identity is essentially independent of institutional roles." Dignity sees the institutional roles relating to gender, ethnicity, or family as obstacles rather than pathways to self-discovery. "The implicit sociology [of dignity]," Berger writes, "views all biological and historical differentiations as either downright unreal or essentially irrelevant.... [T]he individual can only discover his true identity by emancipating himself from his socially enclosed roles—the latter are only masks, entangling him in illusion, alienation, and bad faith."

In a dignity framework, your institutions and roles can conceal one's true self from the individuals themselves. This makes room for the idea of false consciousness. Thus, it can make sense for people in dignity cultures to say, for example, that Muslim women don't *really want* to wear a veil in spite of what they tell outsiders. Or that American women aren't *truly choosing* to be stay-at-home moms even if they say and believe they want to do so. The dignity framework allows for the separation of the true self from an oppressive social structure when that social structure can influence the beliefs and desires of the oppressed.

This idea can have tremendous moral advantages. Many honor cultures do indeed have oppressive social structures that impose restrictions on not just a person's role but also what he or she is permitted to do. In certain cultures, for example, girls are prohibited from getting an education because it is not deemed a woman's proper role. Preventing people from getting educated is a genuine obstacle to self-realization and therefore an infringement of basic human autonomy. In other honor groups, the surrounding environment makes it necessary to adopt a pose or a role even when it doesn't reflect who the person is. Sociologist Elijah Anderson gives a moving account of the struggle that children face in the inner-city neighborhoods of Philadelphia. "As a means of survival," he writes, "one often learns the value of having a 'name,' a reputation for being willing and able to fight." The code of the street imposes this burden on the so-called street kids as well as on the "decent kids"—the ones who don't want to start trouble but just wish to be left alone. The decent kids have to campaign publicly for respect too. Otherwise, they can be ostracized, robbed, assaulted, taken for a punk. Parents encourage aggressive behavior and sometimes punish them for not fighting back against a bully or assailant. Anderson writes that "to avoid being bothered decent and street youths alike must say through behavior, words, and gestures, 'If you mess with me, there will be a severe physical penalty—coming from me. And I'm man enough to make you pay.'" The sad irony to this aspect of the code is that to live a decent, peaceful life, the kids must engage in public displays of aggression. "With the right amount of respect, individuals can avoid being bothered in public." But to get respect, they have to fight back when someone steps up to them.

The same dynamic is found in prisons. I recently spoke to some former inmates who have been through the Prisoner Entrepreneurship Program (PEP), a Texas organization that offers job training and character building for prisoners about to be released. Knowing the environments that most prisoners come from, the program begins with a "degangsterization process," where the inmates give each other "sweet names" (like Candy Corn or Milli Vanilli) to help them shed their former images. "Degangsterization," one prisoner told me, "is really a process of self-discovery.... When you're in prison," he says, "you take on an identity for survival. When you get into PEP, you can find out who *you* are." This is a perfect description of the benefits of moving from an honor to a dignity culture as it relates to identity. By rejecting the primacy of social structures both formal and informal, dignity offers more freedom—indeed, unlimited freedom—for individuals to determine their own values and identities.

But this liberty, like most liberties, comes at a cost. Institutions provide stability and structure. They provide boundaries for people to explore without getting lost. Many of the young men turned to gangs in the first place to find community, stability, and social support that society failed to provide. In prison the inmates have the regimentation of prison life to ground them. As many prisoners report, life can be much harder to navigate post-release. (The PEP program establishes halfway houses and continued job training for ex-cons to ease the transition.) This phenomenon is familiar to people in dignity cultures. With no institutional boundaries, Berger writes, discovering one's identity "becomes the goal of an often devious and difficult quest." Dignity, in other words, offers little guidance for people who want to "find themselves." Without any constraints on identity, people risk getting lost, alienated from the self they now have the freedom to discover. Just as the constraints of an art form can bring out the artist's creativity, the constraints of institutionalized roles can make the project of self-realization more manageable.

Well-functioning honor cultures find ways to balance the structure of imposed roles with enough individual freedom to avoid oppression. An example I'll return to several times in this book is the honor culture of the National Hockey League. A core element of the NHL's honor code is that players understand and embrace their role for the team. The roles determine how the player should behave on the ice. The role of skill players is to generate scoring through shots and assists. The enforcer's role is to intimidate opponents and protect his teammates from taking cheap shots. The role of the "agitators" is to get under their opponent's skin, to probe for weakness or make them lose their cool. The code demands that players accept their roles and not stray from them. As enforcer Don Cherry puts it, "The crusher who becomes a rusher [to score] soon becomes an usher." Accept who you are, in other words, or your new role will be to serve beer to the fans.

The players don't just accept their roles to stay in the league, however. And they don't regard them as veils or disguises that conceal their "true identity" as hockey players. The roles allow them to discover their identity as hockey players. They take pride in excelling at them. Enforcer Jeff Odgers describes it like this:

As kids we all had visions of being the guy who was on the power play and who scored that big goal in overtime. That is what we all strived for. But as you get older and wiser, you realize some of your limitations, where your skill level was, and what you could bring to the table. At a certain point you come to the realization that if you want to make it in this league you have to adapt and embrace whatever role the coaches have in mind for you. For me that was being a tough guy. No, it wasn't as sexy as being a goal scorer, but it was my ticket to play and I was able to do so for a pretty long time. I just wanted to be in the NHL more than anything in my life, and that is how I was able to make my dream come true. I didn't love fighting, but I did enjoy being respected and liked by my teammates for protecting them. There is great honor in that.

Odgers is not showing bad faith; the remarks demonstrate no false consciousness. Odgers recognizes that he is working within externally imposed constraints. But he also understands that it is precisely these constraints that enable him to gain honor and to realize who he is as a hockey player.

This connection between identity and institutional roles is found in many honor subcultures, like the military, the Mafia, and urban gang culture. The sharply defined roles provide structure and norms of behavior for members. The rigidity of the roles varies according to the group, and almost all have some flexibility. But they do not have unlimited flexibility and therefore do not provide unlimited autonomy. Of course, the same is true for nonhonor cultures as well. We all have biologically and socially imposed limits on what we can do. What distinguishes honor and nonhonor societies is the way they understand these limits—as veils or obstacles to self-discovery or as an indispensable means of forming one's identity.

This might sound rather abstract, but as we've seen, identification leads to action. Since honor can constrain identity, it may also constrain the behaviors that we're motivated to perform. So let's examine the norms of behavior in honor groups to get a better sense of the actions that honor's elaborate network of incentives typically motivates.

Honor Norms

First things first: What's a norm? Norms are the rules or principles that govern human behavior within society. Every known society has norms, and human beings have an innate capacity for acquiring and internalizing them. Children learn the norms of their society early in life and get scolded or punished when they violate them. As norms are internalized, they become tied to certain emotions. We feel anger when others violate group norms (especially moral norms) and guilt or shame when we violate them. Society has a variety of mechanisms for enforcing its norms of behavior. Some are formal, like legal punishment. Others are informal, such as shaming, gossip, and ostracism.

Some norms are human universals. Every known society has a norm that requires parents to care and provide for their children. Other norms are local to a specific culture and might seem bizarre to people in a different culture. If you travel to Iran, for example, you'll encounter *taarof,* a cluster of norms around politeness and respect. As an honored visitor, your taxi driver might offer to provide your ride for free. *Taarof* requires that you refuse and insist on paying and then for the driver to repeat the offer and again for you to refuse. After a few more rounds of offers and refusals, the driver will allow you to pay the fare. Similarly, if you're invited to someone's home and offered food, *taarof* dictates that you decline, no matter how hungry you are. After they insist a few times, then you can accept it.

The principles of *taarof* can be categorized as honor norms because they are concerned with matters of respect and deference. What are some other typical honor norms? For the most part, the answer depends on the honor group we're talking about. The norms of the Albanian highlanders don't have much in common with the norms of stand-up comics or the norms of the Victorian aristocracy. That said, we can identify some norms that most, if not all, honor societies have in common. Hospitality is one of them. One of the most common features of honor codes across cultures and throughout history is a strong focus on the guest-host relationship. You probably know that the cause of the Trojan War was Paris absconding with Helen, the wife of Menelaus. What you may not know is that Paris's act was regarded as an offense against hospitality. Guests as well as hosts have obligations, and Paris violated his in dramatic fashion. Zeus, the most powerful of the Greek gods, is in fact the god of *xenia*—or hospitality. And since Paris was a Trojan prince, Zeus decreed that the Greeks would win the war.

Hospitality remains of central importance in honor cultures today. If you've traveled widely, chances are you've received the warmest welcomes in countries characterized as honor cultures, and it can be a shock returning home to a society without the same commitment to hospitality. In modern rural Greece, the person who shows hospitality to strangers brings credit to the entire household. To the bedouin, hospitality norms are intimately connected to a family's honor and reputation. When bedouin invite a stranger into a tent or building for coffee, tea, and food, "the guest is protected from harm, and thus rearticulates social customs by creating a 'moral space,' in which the guest is treated as a member of the 'house.'"

Hospitality imposes its share of burdens as well. The Balgawi in Jordan say that "the host must fear his guest. When he sits [and shares your food], he is company. When he stands [and leaves your house], he is a poet"—meaning that he can broadcast how he was treated to the rest of the honor group. Reputations are at stake: "With subtle remarks on lukewarm tea, paltry servings of meat, reluctant greetings, or farewells given too easily, 'poets' can tarnish the name of hosts who offend them." The obligations of hospitality persist even when they put the host in physical danger. The ancient codes of the Pashtun tribes include the principle of *lokhay warkawal*, which binds the tribe to safeguard and protect their guest from an enemy at all costs, even at risk to their own lives. Navy SEAL Marcus Luttrell, subject of the book and film *Lone Survivor*, owes his life to the Pashtun norms of hospitality.

So central is the commitment to hospitality in some cultures that it can lead to violent feuds. Writer Ismail Kadare's fascinating novel *Broken April* tells the story of a young Albanian highlander, Georg, trapped in a multigenerational feud with a rival family. The

feud began seventy years earlier, long before Georg was born, when
a stranger happened to pass by Georg's grandfather's house in the
evening. The grandfather welcomed him in, offered him food and
shelter, and then escorted him to the outer limits of the village. The
grandfather then turned to go home and heard a shot. The stranger,
involved in a feud of his own, had been killed. Since the body happened to fall facedown toward the village, the victim was still tech-
nically the grandfather's guest. So according to the Albanian codes
of hospitality, the grandfather and his family were now bound to
avenge his death by killing a member of the shooter's clan. (Had
he fallen facing away from the village, they would have had no such
duty.) By the time the novel's protagonist, Georg, is drawn into the
feud, forty-four people have been murdered, twenty-two from each
family.

Although it is a work of fiction, Kadare's story gives an accurate account of Albanian honor norms, as described in the *Kanun*,
a collection of customary laws that cover all aspects of the Albanian
highlanders' social and economic life. A stranger falling at a certain
angle can lead to a bloodbath. In the *Kanun*, the guest represents
"the supreme ethical category, more important than blood relations."
The guest in Albania is like a demigod. Once you invite one into
your house, you become responsible for his safety. If he is harmed
on your property, you incur a debt of honor to avenge the wrong—
even if both victim and offender are strangers. It is a striking and
somewhat puzzling fact about honor cultures that so many of them
take the obligations of hospitality to such extremes.

Another common set of honor norms is one I alluded to in the opening of this chapter: the obligations to stand up personally against challenges, insults, and signs of disrespect—even when that comes with significant risk. This value is so central to honor that some scholars regard it as defining. "At root," says William Ian Miller, "honor means 'don't tread on me.'" A man of honor, writes ex-mafioso Bill Bonanno, "is someone willing to acknowledge the power of another . . . but he is not willing to brook an insult to his own honor in that relationship." Backing down from a challenge in honor cultures frequently has negative consequences. People use insults to probe for weakness and climb the ladder of vertical honor. If you challenge someone and they don't respond, you gain honor at their expense. But pragmatic considerations like this are only part of the story. It is a source of profound shame to back down from a challenge in honor cultures—independent of anything that may come from doing so. Most people in dignity cultures can relate to these feelings to some extent at least. How often have you lain in bed going over all the things you *should* have said to that person who slighted you at work, or a bar, or the gym? But for most of us, these feelings are fleeting and superficial—they might cause us to blush from discomfort for a couple of days, but then we get over it. They don't cut right to the core of our sense of self-respect and self-worth. Again, the difference is one of degree, but it is a crucial difference.

The respective norms for handling conflict in honor and dignity cultures reflect a broader, more theoretical distinction between the concepts of honor and dignity. Honor is tenuous and fragile, and it has to be preserved and defended with vigilance. Dignity, by contrast, is stable and enduring. At least in theory, we all have dignity simply by virtue of being human—and nobody can take it away. Dignity is like the participation trophy my daughter got after her team went 0–12 in her basketball league. Everyone gets one; it doesn't matter whether you win or lose or even how you played the game. As legal scholar Orit Kamir describes it, dignity "follows no norms of conduct and is measured against no standards of achievement.... [I]t involves no competition and no rivalry.... [N]othing a person does or refrains from doing can enhance or endanger his or her human dignity."

Under this (admittedly idealized) conception of dignity, you don't need to defend your self-worth against challenges or insults because your self-worth, by definition, cannot be diminished in the first place. Consequently, dignity does not require or even tolerate personal or private responses to offenses. When someone is wronged, dignity regards it "not [as] an affront to the individual" but rather as "an affront to the whole family, humankind, and its self-determined collective worth." Consequently, the duty to respond to the affront falls not on the individual but on humankind as a whole. In practice, of course, matters may be quite different. But this ideal has had massive implications—both good and bad, as we'll see—for society. It has reshaped the way in which people in dignity cultures relate to one another and transformed the modern understanding of punishment. Indeed, this concept of dignity is at the heart of our criminal justice system. When someone commits a criminal offense, the trial isn't one between the victim and the offender. It becomes a conflict between the offender and "the people," the offender and "the state." The victims' identities, and their desires and wishes, are deemed irrelevant. (Much more on this in Chapter Six.)

Honor takes precisely the opposite view. After an insult, writes Bill Bonanno about the Sicilian honor culture, "no one steps up and demands justice—only revenge. And that act is personal, private and passionate. Yet it is the heart and soul of an entire people [the Sicilians]." In an honor framework, when someone challenges your self-worth, humankind isn't abused; *you* are. Accordingly, the obligation to address the challenge falls on you, and maybe your family or group, and not on humankind. If you fail to do so, you lose honor and risk being shamed, disgraced, and even excluded from the group—as poor Sean Tracey learned the hard way. Not surprisingly, honor cultures tend to be suspicious and even hostile to third-party "impartial" justice. External interference strips the offended parties of their chance to stand up for themselves, to demonstrate courage, and most of all to affirm their self-worth against the offenses. This aversion to third-party involvement is present in a variety of honor cultures: urban gangs have "stop snitching" campaigns; baseball players don't involve the league office in their feuds; Algerians find prison to be a "nuisance," an annoying delay on the path to *real* justice.

Relatedly, people in honor cultures typically show a heightened sensitivity to insults—and are quick to retaliate at the first sign of disrespect. In a classic paper on honor and dignity, sociologist Peter Berger writes that honor's obsolescence in the modern West is "revealed very sharply in the inability of most contemporaries to understand insult, which in essence is an assault on honor." Modern Americans, Berger observes, don't regard insults as genuine harms unless they lead to tangible harms, such as a loss of income or career prospects. Steven Pinker illustrates this attitude in his sardonic description of the centuries-old practice of dueling. The participants, he writes, "were fighting not for money or land or even women but for honor, the strange commodity that exists because everyone believes that everyone else believes that it exists." From this perspective, it might make sense to fight a duel over money or land or women, because those things are tangible and material and therefore real. But honor? That makes no sense at all. This attitude is both baffling and shameful to people in honor cultures. They regard their reputation, their honor, as their most treasured possession, far more important than money or property.

Most problematic for people like me who wish to defend honor are the norms for female modesty and purity. Many honor cultures, though by no means all of them, impose strict codes of chastity and fidelity for their female members. Violating the codes can lead to shame, ostracizing, physical punishment, even murder in extreme cases—the so-called "honor killings" one finds in some communities. Fortunately, honor killings are at the far extreme end of the spectrum—the vast majority of honor cultures do not endorse murdering relatives for having extramarital sex. But the burdens of honor can fall on women in many shades or degrees. Some studies suggest that honor cultures in Latin America are more likely to be tolerant of domestic violence against women who are unfaithful to their partners. Men with unfaithful spouses are perceived as less manly, less honorable—which gives them all the more reason to closely monitor their partners' behavior. In his classic ethnography of rural Greece, J. K. Campbell writes that a woman is expected to have "sexual shame," which is a "revulsion from sexual activity, an attempt in dress, movement, and attitude, to disguise the fact that she possesses the physical attributes of her sex." The burden for women is significant, making them afraid of even false accusations of "sexual misbehavior." Campbell also notes the connection between female purity and the man's honor. Suspicion of a woman's impurity "always implicates the honor of the men in the family, reflecting on the manliness of the husband, and, more generally, on the whole social personality of brothers and, particularly, sons....[T]he women must have shame if the manliness of their men is not to be dishonored." The result is a kind of feedback loop to enforce female purity and fidelity. Norms are in place to shame both women for violations and also their male family members, which gives the males an additional incentive to keep a close eye on their female kin.

We shouldn't underestimate the freedom and power women possess in these cultures. In a more recent ethnography of rural Greek cultures, anthropologist Jill Dubisch writes that women were "hardly the downtrodden, submissive and self-effacing beings that accounts such as Campbell's would have had me believe." Dubisch continues: "Not surprisingly, there were differences among individuals as well—women who were dominated by their husbands and fit more with the 'Mediterranean woman' stereotype, and women who bullied their spouses, and ran their households with a firm hand, as well as households in which the husband's show of masculine dominance was regarded with amused tolerance by the wife. And in many, if not most cases, these village women exhibited a self-confidence that I sometimes envied."

Still, the apparent connection between honor and the mistreatment of women is troubling. Not surprisingly, it's also the most common objection I get from people when I tell them what I'm writing about. I raised the issue in my interviews with William Ian Miller (an expert on honor cultures and saga Iceland) and Anthony Appiah (author of *The Honor Code*), both of whom have wrestled with it in their own work. Miller believes that the connection between honor and female chastity is overstated. "What about an honor culture like my saga Iceland guys," he asks me, "who couldn't give a damn about whether their women screwed around?" According to Miller, the honor killings that one finds in some Islamic and Hindu communities have nothing to do with honor; rather, they have to do with "the underlying norms about which they decide that honor are at stake." Miller is right, as far as that theory goes. Still, it does seem to be a running theme in many honor cultures, and the prevalence of these attitudes demands an explanation.

When I put this same question to Appiah, his reply was illuminating. "It's just a complex social psychological fact that honor is one of the mechanisms that gets mobilized to police gender and sexuality," he told me. "When things are of value or important to you, honor is going to be one of the mechanisms you employ to support them." Men want their women to be faithful. Human beings in general have a special concern for female fidelity. And sex norms are especially difficult to enforce, because sexual behavior is tempting and typically takes place in the absence of witnesses. The stricter the sexual codes are, the more difficult they will be to enforce. Honor isn't the source of the codes, but it often gets recruited for enforcing them, because of its general motivational effectiveness and the way it gets people to internalize social norms. Now, to be clear: This is a purely descriptive and historical story. It does not in any way morally justify strict codes of sexual purity for women. What it reveals is the absence of a *necessary* connection between the idea of honor and sexist norms and practices. Changing morally odious norms doesn't require doing away with honor. But the story does not exempt honor for its contribution to gender subjection either. On the contrary, once in place, immoral honor codes can be proximate mechanisms for oppression.

So let's take stock. Honor can lead to long, bloody cycles of violence between families that are sparked by something as arbitrary as the angle a stranger falls to the ground. It can force children trying to lead decent, law-abiding lives to act tough and aggressively just to be left alone. Honor can trap individuals within rigid social roles, limiting their autonomy as rational agents to determine their own identity and conception of a good life. Honor has no essential commitment to universal human rights, and in some communities honor is the mechanism for systematic violations of the rights of women. That's a lot of baggage. Meanwhile, the concept of dignity has brought tremendous benefits. It has provided the philosophical foundation for a universal conception of individual liberty and equal treatment. Its aim is to provide all human beings, no matter how

lowly born or disadvantaged, with real value and the freedom to determine who they are and what they do. Maybe the critics are right
that we're better off rejecting honor in favor of dignity.

I take these criticisms very seriously. Without question, any defense of honor must address them. I have three replies that I'll examine in detail over the remainder of the book. The first is simply
to point out that although honor has no necessary commitment to
human rights, it is not incompatible with such a commitment either. The idea that it is incompatible is a common misconception
that prevents many critics from evaluating the costs and benefits of
honor with an open mind. Celebrated anthropologist and sociologist Pierre Bourdieu, for example, writes that "the ethos of honor is
fundamentally opposed to a universal and formal morality which affirms the equality in dignity of all men and consequently the equality of their rights and duties." The dictates of honor, according to
Bourdieu, are directly applied to the individual case and vary according to the situation. Thus, "they are in no way capable of being made
universal. This is so much the case that a single system of values of
honor establishes two opposing sets of rules of conduct—on the
one hand that which governs relationships between kinsmen and in
general all personal relations that conform to the same pattern as
those between kinsmen; and on the other hand that which is valid
in one's relationships with strangers." Like many of honor's critics,
Bourdieu confuses two distinct positions: an opposition to universal
and formal morality and a failure to respect human rights and equality. Bourdieu is right that honor norms and values tend to be culture
specific, constantly changing, with no pretense to universality. People

in honor cultures believe that their norms apply to the members of their own group, not to all human beings, persons, rational agents, or God's children. (As we'll see, this can be a tremendous advantage to honor frameworks.) But honor's indifference to formal, abstract universal ethical systems does not rule out a respect for basic human rights. Democracy, after all, was born in the Mediterranean honor culture of ancient Greece. Honor values did not prevent the modern Renaissance of Italy and Spain. And the strong commitment to family and communal honor in modern Japan has contributed to the success of its educational and economic systems. "What Japan, and indeed portions of the Middle East, shows," writes cultural psychologist Gary Gregg, "is that familial attachments and sentiments of honor can fuel achievement, entrepreneurialship, and modernization *under auspicious conditions.*" Now, it's true that sometimes conditions in honor cultures are inauspicious and that some honor cultures violate these rights on a daily basis. It's also true that some cultures justify these violations—honor killings, for example—by appealing to honor's demands. What this reveals, however, is that the morality of honor is incomplete, not that we should reject it entirely. Honor needs external boundaries, constraints on behavior, that are not themselves derived from the principles of honor. One of these constraints is a respect for human rights. Fortunately, as we'll see, plenty of well-functioning honor cultures accept this basic commitment.

My second reply is that honor's robust motivational structure can be recruited to bring about desired moral change—including human rights violations. Just as honor is an effective tool for norm enforcement, it is also an effective tool for norm transformation—and for the same reasons. As Appiah shows in his book, for example, honor played a crucial role in bringing the cruel thousand-year-old practice of foot binding in China to an end. It's true that the concept of dignity is often employed to demonstrate the injustice of such practices. But dignity provides few psychological resources for bringing about the desired moral change. Honor has these resources to spare. By identifying the auspicious conditions for honor to function, we can harness its motivational power and psychological insights. Honor can be a problem in societies with immoral norms and attitudes, but it can also be a big part of the solution.

Third, I'll suggest that the moral self-congratulation of dignity cultures is premature and that dignity often works much better in theory than in practice. Just as honor can impose burdens and costs to society, rejecting honor does as well. The next chapter examines several of the biggest costs: hyper risk aversion, a growing lack of community and solidarity, and diminished personal accountability. These troubling phenomena only get worse with each passing year, and they are the direct result of our collective rejection of honor in favor of dignity. Let's turn to that discussion now.

CHAPTER 2

LIVING WITHOUT HONOR

As anyone who knows me will confirm (usually rolling their eyes), I'm on a crusade against bicycle helmets. I don't wear them, I don't make my daughter wear one, and I get enraged on rides when some spandex-covered cyclist starts lecturing me on the risks of head injuries. I'll recognize the irony if I get paralyzed from a bike accident, but I'll regret nothing. Because I'm not just opposed to bike helmets. I'm morally opposed to them.

You might reasonably wonder why I'm waging this war against bike helmets. Is it because of the studies that reveal the risks of failing to wear one to be inflated and that in fact motorists drive slightly closer to bikers who wear helmets, marginally increasing the threat of an accident? No, absolutely not. My opposition runs much deeper than that. Again, it's a moral issue. To me, bicycle helmets represent many of the most shameful and tragic problems of modern life. I believe you can draw a direct link between bike helmets and the drug war, police militarization, mass incarceration, drone warfare, and the Syrian refugee ban. If you wear a bicycle helmet, I tell people, then you support the Syrian refugee ban. It's that simple. My friends and colleagues can't tell if I'm joking. I'm not joking. Okay, maybe I'm exaggerating a little, but I'm not joking.

There's a serious point here. When you force people to wear something uncomfortable (and dorky) because of an insignificant safety benefit, people are significantly less inclined to ride bikes. This reduces their quality of life. The massive increases in helmet-wearing regulations, standards, and norms are indicative of ever-increasing risk aversion in society, a phenomenon with devastating moral and practical consequences. Of course, bike helmets are not the cause of this phenomenon; they are just another symptom. As I'll argue in this chapter, rejecting honor has in large part brought this about. Obviously, you don't have to have an honor orientation to have a sensible attitude toward bike helmets. (You can just be European.) But hyper risk-averse attitudes are possible only in a society that has rejected honor. And this risk aversion is one of the biggest and most neglected costs of casting honor aside as a core value.

Risk aversion isn't the only unfortunate consequence of rejecting honor—diminishing personal accountability, increasing social isolation, alienation, and a weakening sense of solidarity and community spirit have all followed too. A word of warning: This is the grumpy chapter. This is the cranky "get-off-my-lawn," "kids these days," "society is going to hell" part of the book. When I shopped around the book proposal, one editor asked me to make this part predominant, with a title like "Americans Are a Big Bunch of Cowards," and to have an alarmist shaming quality running through the argument.

But I wasn't interested in that. For one thing, it's just not my temperament to be that angry (except when someone lectures me about helmets). For another: I'm genuinely not generally pessimistic about society and the modern character. Don't get me wrong—I think the rise in risk aversion is a serious problem. But I don't think the problems run that deep in our natures. As we'll see in the later chapters of this book, the frameworks and structures of honor subcultures can bring out the best in people even when the larger culture stays as it is. Honor, in other words, has the resources to push back against many of the damaging by-products of modern life.

But first I need to convince you that risk aversion, diminished solidarity, and reduced personal accountability are genuinely regrettable developments. And they are brought about, at least in part, by the flagging commitment to honor in the West. Let's turn to that now.

Home of the Cowardly

Americans are obsessed with personal safety. We're not rational about it, of course—if we really wanted to stop risking our lives, we wouldn't get into cars. But our conscious goal in personal conduct and national policy is to minimize all threats to life and limb. Okay, fine, you might say. What's wrong with erring on the side of safety? The answer is that living a good and moral life is impossible without the courage to take risks.

Here's one example: On January 7, 2015, al-Qaida gunmen broke into the office of the satirical newspaper *Charlie Hebdo* with automatic weapons. They murdered twelve people. The gunmen claimed to be avenging Muhammad, retaliating against the newspaper for publishing disrespectful images of the Prophet. The Koran, according to some interpretations, prohibits all images of Muhammad.

After the attacks, the slogan *"Je suis Charlie"* went viral on social media, a means of showing solidarity with the murder victims. Meanwhile, major media outlets were facing a test. How should they cover the story? Should they print the allegedly offensive *Charlie Hebdo* cartoons, the ones that provoked the attack? The news media's job is to cover a story, and the cartoons were at the center of the story, no question about that. On the other hand, look what happened in Paris—it might be a little risky to publish the cartoons in their articles. For most major news outlets, the latter considerations trumped the former: they opted not to the print the cartoons in the immediate aftermath of the attack.

And then there was *Charlie Hebdo*. Just a few days after nearly half of their own staff had been gunned down, a skeleton crew of surviving members released their next issue. On the cover was the headline *"Tout est pardoné"* (All is forgiven) and a cartoon picture of a tearful Muhammad holding up a sign saying *"Je suis Charlie."* It was a supremely brave act of defiance, a proud group of journalists refusing to back down in the face of genuine peril.

Now the news media faced *another* test. This was a new development in the story, so how should they report it? Surely, they would be shamed into printing the new *Charlie Hebdo* cover in their own papers, right? Wrong. Even after the release of the new issue, major American media outlets—among them CNN, ABC, the *New York Times*, the Associated Press, and more—opted not to publish images of the new cover. It was a stunning display of spinelessness and a betrayal of their function as news organizations.

The cowardice of these media is even more objectionable when you consider that by failing to publish the cartoons, they increased the risk of the organizations that chose to do their jobs and publish them. Think about it. Islamic terrorists had just murdered journalists in retaliation for printing those images. Editors at the major newspapers that printed the images, such as the *Washington Post*, the *Los Angeles Times*, and *USA Today*, were probably a little concerned and afraid too. But they published the cartoons, because newspapers are supposed to give a complete and accurate account of a story.

A similar dilemma occurred ten years earlier in 2005 after the Danish journal *Jyllands-Posten* published deliberately provocative cartoons of Muhammad, causing violent Muslim protests across the world. Before the protests, the news media showed no reluctance to publish Muhammad's image. But once the prospect of danger appeared, the media abandoned their journalistic mission and put their fellow journalists in peril. By bowing to fear and intimidation, blogger Allahpundit wrote, the Western media "painted the bullseye on Charlie Hebdo for jihadis by their refusal." *Charlie Hebdo* was a target precisely because it was one of the very few organizations committed to its mission—in their case, as a satirical journal. The *Times*'s decision (and that of the Associated Press, CNN, ABC, and many others) had consequences beyond the paper's own journalistic failures.

It may sound paradoxical, but today we place too much value on our own lives. Threats to physical safety, no matter how infinitesimal, have come to trump all other concerns, moral and otherwise. This obsession with risk is antithetical to honor, which places supreme importance on courage and being faithful to your group's principles. In Chapter One, I mentioned the story of Marcus Luttrell, the navy SEAL who found himself alone in Afghan enemy territory after an ambush by Taliban fighters. Luttrell almost certainly would have been captured or killed if he hadn't come across a Pashtun tribe, who offered him *lokhay warkawal*. In Luttrell's words, the term means "an unbreakable commitment to defend that wounded man to the death. And not just the death of the principal tribesman or family who made the original commitment.... It means the whole damned village. Lokhay means the population of that village will fight to the last man, honor-bound to protect the individual they have invited in to share their hospitality. And this is not something to have a chitchat about when things get rough. It's not a point of renegotiation. This is strictly nonnegotiable." The tribespeople knowingly risked their lives—and the danger wasn't negligible—to protect Luttrell from the Taliban, who were ostensibly their allies and rulers of the nation in which they resided. Why? Because their honor required them to do so.

Compare the tribespeople's attitude to our own cowardly unwillingness to help Syrian refugees. After the 2015 ISIS attacks in Paris that killed 130 people, US governors and presidential candidates tripped over themselves to announce they would ban the settling of more refugees. Donald Trump, of course, used the incident to inflame the panic of the American people and continues to do so after every attack. But it's not just Trump. At least twenty-six state governors announced they were closing off their states to the desperate people, who were themselves fleeing from ISIS. Tough-talking Chris Christie announced that New Jersey would turn away three-year-old orphans. Texas senator Ted Cruz called Obama's intent to honor the US commitment nothing short of crazy. "It would be the height of foolishness," Cruz said, "to bring in tens of thousands of people, including jihadists who are coming here to murder innocent Americans." Not to be outdone, Texas governor Greg Abbott tweeted this: "BREAKING: Texas will not accept any Syrian refugees & I demand the U.S. act similarly. Security comes first."

As a proud transplant to Houston, I was embarrassed. The governor of the swashbuckling state of Texas wanted to turn away families fleeing from ISIS in the name of "security." Security from what? There had been exactly zero terrorist incidents caused by Islamic refugees in America. Refugees go through extensive screening and are significantly less likely than American citizens to commit crimes. None of these details matters, though, if avoiding risks—no matter how negligible—is your number-one priority.

After the Paris attacks, the French president, François Hollande, announced his country would accept *more* Syrian refugees, upping the total from twenty-four to thirty thousand. "France should remain as it is," Hollande said. "Our duty is to carry on our lives." For all the jokes about the French penchant for surrendering, they stood tall while America surrendered its principles—and all because of an attack on French soil! Regarding Hollande's statement, columnist

Michael Tomasky wrote, "Imagine an American president making a similar announcement five days after a terrorist attack on New York or Washington! He'd be crucified." But here's the thing: I'm not sure Tomasky is right about that. The problem is that our leaders don't even try.

It's true that not everyone in the United States opposed accepting more refugees. But the whole debate is impoverished, because we have no recourse to the language of honor. The politicians who favor accepting refugees often appeal to moral considerations—claiming that it's our duty to accept people who are in desperate need of help. But these arguments fail to persuade; opponents insist we have a greater moral duty to protect our own citizens. Others appeal to rational probability calculations to the insignificant threats that refugees pose. But while it's certainly irrational to be scared of refugees, overwhelming research in social science has demonstrated that people simply aren't rational when it comes to probability calculations. Appealing to such calculations alone has little motivational effect. But why not in addition appeal to the honor of the American people? Why not say, "Okay, yes. It's possible that accepting them poses a tiny threat, but these refugees need our help. They're fleeing from the most brutal regime imaginable. It's *shameful*, cowardly, not to bear the negligible risk that the wrong person will make it through. We're not cowards; we're Americans. We've always had the courage to support people in great distress, and there is no reason to change that now." We've lost the power of such appeals because we've abandoned the language of honor. The rhetoric surrounding dignity is mostly about noninterference, respecting the rights of others. But

Syrian refugees don't need us not to interfere with their rights. They need help. For cases like a refugee crisis in another nation, honor gives us a voice when dignity has nothing to say.

I'm aware that economic and political interests often favor stirring panic in the nation. But that doesn't let us off the hook. Politicians and the media benefit only by exacerbating fears that are already there. Scare tactics wouldn't work very well in a country of people who take pride in their courage, who regard their willingness to face danger as part of their identity. In that culture, news networks wouldn't get high ratings for hyping the latest shark attack or virus that has affected .0004 percent of the population.

This epidemic of risk aversion is pervasive throughout our culture. Consider how we raise our children. We teach them to fear strangers when the likelihood of being kidnapped by a nonrelative is vanishingly small. We ban playground equipment for being too dangerous, strap our children into car seats more suitable to Hannibal Lecter during a prison transfer, and hover over them like jealous spouses, never giving them unsupervised time to learn how to handle threats themselves. On several occasions, parents have been arrested for letting their children play alone at a park—only to be reported to the police by a "concerned" stranger. A countermovement called "free-range children" has emerged to push back against parental hysteria. But again, without recourse to honor language, the debate suffers, focusing only on the numbers. Steven Pinker, for example, defends the "free-range children" movement by saying the following: "The annual number of abductions by strangers has ranged from 200 or 300 in the 1990s to about 100 today, about half of whom are murdered. With 50 million children in the United States, that works out to an annual homicide rate of one in a million.... That's about a twentieth of the risk of drowning and a fortieth of the risk of a fatal car accident."

Pinker is right, of course, but not persuasive: the argument has minimal emotional force. Again, human beings are notoriously inept when it comes to processing high numbers and tiny probabilities. One shark attack in ten years is enough to make us stay away from that beach forever. Pinker could make a far more compelling case by emphasizing the importance of raising tough, self-reliant, courageous children. Unfortunately, those are the "fetishized virtues" that Pinker had complained about earlier in his book.

More perversely, psychologist Ryan Brown considers the new risk aversion to be an enormous advantage—and he makes it a centerpiece of his case against the "honor syndrome." Brown conducts research to show that accidental deaths are slightly higher in so-called honor states (mostly in the American South) than in non-honor states. The percentages are minuscule in both. He also shows that both men and women with a greater honor orientation score higher on a scale for risky attitudes and behavior. When Dallas writer Lucy Adams took issue with his honor bashing, Brown replied as follows: "As a social scientist, I go where the data take me whether it's to pleasant or unpleasant places. Behaviors associated with honor ideologies are more frequently of the latter type.... It is the job of academics like me... to discover reality, using evidence and systematic analysis, rather than relying on anecdotes viewed through the lens of cultural ideologies." It's a revealing passage. Like so many morally minded scientists who claim to just "follow the data," Brown is blind to his own implicit value judgments. Here is what his evidence and "systematic analysis" revealed: people who endorsed an honor ideology were, among other things, more likely to engage in "excessive risk-taking." What kind of risk taking does Brown deem to be (objectively) excessive? Activities like "bungee-jumping," "camping in the wilderness," "swimming far out from shore on an unguarded lake or ocean," "taking a sky-diving class," "piloting a small plane," and "walking home alone at night in an unsafe area of town."

This is the typical MO of many honor critics, presenting controversial (and in this case misguided) value judgments as empirical fact. Brown's unspoken assumption is that we ought to live in a way that maximizes the probability of a long life, no matter the cost. An experience like bungee jumping or backcountry camping or skydiving is deemed "excessively" or "irrationally" risky because it marginally increases the probability of an early death. But what if activities like backcountry camping and skydiving and scuba diving and others are part of what makes life worth living in the first place? A sense of adventure is not a vice; it's a virtue. Imagine how impoverished your life would be if you systematically excluded any behavior that carried the slightest threat of physical harm. No wonder stories about honor stir the public imagination! Many of us recognize and connect with the spirit of adventure, even as we sense it receding in our own experience.

Now, look—maybe you have no interest in bungee jumping, skydiving, or camping in the wilderness. Maybe you're comfortable with your current level of adventure and risk. That's fine. But still, the moral considerations against obsessing about risk are overwhelming. These attitudes have ushered in the age of military policing, the Patriot Act, domestic spying, Guantánamo, three-strikes-and-you're-out laws, zero-tolerance schooling, the school-to-prison pipeline, and a secret drone program, among many other tragic and immoral developments. None of these institutions and policies would be politically feasible in a more courageous culture.

Let's say you agree. There's another question: How can we reverse course? Aversion to physical threat is natural. Human beings have an innate survival instinct that isn't calibrated to the minimal everyday dangers of the modern world. Sticking to our moral principles in the face of a perceived threat is difficult. It requires deep shame when we back down and fierce pride when we don't. And here's where honor can help. Honor cultures of every sort place deep value on courage and personal integrity. As we saw in Chapter One, honor provides strong positive incentives to act courageously (to improve your standing—your *time* within the group) and negative incentives for chickening out (shaming, disgrace, loss of *time*, potential loss of horizontal honor). And not merely physical courage but moral courage too. As Sharon Krause argues, a sense of honor helped motivate people like Elizabeth Cady Stanton, Susan B. Anthony, and Martin Luther King Jr. to fight for equality against serious opposition. We'll look at some more detailed examples in Chapter Four. Other sources of motivation, such as material self-interest, legal punishment, morality, and guilt, are much less effective at getting people to overcome their fear. In honor cultures, people strive to be worthy of their status and reputation and to live by an internalized code of conduct. They feel a heightened sense of shame when they fail to do so. Nonhonor cultures lack these motivational resources. It's no accident that virtually all warrior cultures and martial societies employ honor as a central value. But you don't have to be from a warrior culture to appreciate the benefits, moral and otherwise, of a more courageous society.

Home of the Solitary

If the previous section didn't convince you to rethink our safety fetish, then consider too that it's not an isolated phenomenon; it has connections to another troubling modern development: rampant individualism. Author Sebastian Junger in his excellent book *Tribe* offers a nice illustration of how the two phenomena are related. Junger describes his childhood in the comfortable, privileged town of Belmont, outside of Boston. "The predictability of life in an American suburb," Junger writes, "left me hoping—somewhat irresponsibly—for a hurricane or a tornado or something that would require us to all band together to survive." This wasn't a nihilistic urge; Junger didn't want destruction or mayhem. He wanted solidarity: "I wanted the chance to prove my worth to my community and my peers, but I lived in a time and a place where nothing dangerous ever really happened....How do you become an adult in a society that doesn't ask for sacrifice? How do you become a man in a world that doesn't require courage?"

Our sense of community is reignited in times of adversity. Many of us have experienced this. After the 9/11 attacks, American flags went up all across the country. People waited in line for hours to donate blood. After a few days, the Red Cross had to issue a statement that the banks were full and that people should donate later. But as soon as the immediate threat faded, the flags came down and the blood banks were depleted.

Social bonds are reinforced under conditions of adversity and risk, and people are motivated to act for the good of the community rather than themselves. The causal chain goes both ways: lack of solidarity also makes us less courageous. As Bruxeius, a character in Steven Pressfield's *Gates of Fire* about the Battle of Thermopylae, puts it: "Only gods and heroes can be brave in isolation. A man may call upon courage only one way, in the ranks with his brothers-in-arms, the line of his tribe and his city.…No one may expect valor from one cast out alone, cut off from the gods of his home."

Large, anonymous atomized societies like ours struggle with isolation and lack of community, a trend that sociologists have written about for centuries. You can choose your favorite example. Here's one: in Canada, the United Kingdom, and the United States, people have started marrying themselves—a practice known as "sologamy." It's a form of "self-empowerment," expressing to others that you don't need to have a partner in order to be happy. But such gestures transparently protest too much. Human beings are social creatures by nature—we crave bonds and connections with others. We want to live for something larger than ourselves and our material possessions. Unfortunately, the forces of modern life seem hell-bent on making us more and more alone.

The great nineteenth-century sociologist Ferdinand Tonnies distinguished between two types of social relations. The first—*gemeinschaft*—is sometimes translated as "community" but like many German words has no good translation. People who relate in this way regard themselves as part of the community whose value can't be reduced to its individual parts. They have common goals and values, and they don't make a clean distinction between what's good for them as individuals and what's good for the group as a whole. Examples of *gemeinschaft* include the family, army units, sports teams, and religious communities. Within these groups, there is plenty of competition among individuals. But they are working for a common purpose and share some basic standards for how to evaluate people's behavior and characters.

Tonnies contrasts *gemeinschaft* with another type of social relation that best characterizes the modern industrialized West, *gesellschaft*. Whereas in *gemeinschaft* people share a common identity in spite of their individual distinctions, in *gesellschaft* they remain distinct despite their connections as a community or nation. Emile Durkheim describes *gesellschaft* societies as "a circle of men who... live and dwell in peace...but instead of being essentially joined are essentially separate." Cooperation is regulated by market forces. "Nobody is able to make anything for another," Durkheim writes, "unless it is in exchange for a similar service or for a compensation that he judges to be equivalent to that which he has given." Sociologist Robert Nisbett adds that *gesellschaft* is "characterized by a high degree of individualism, impersonality, [and] contractualism, that proceed

from volition or sheer interest rather than from the complex of af-
fective states, habits, and traditions that underlies *gemeinschaft*." In
the place of tradition and unconscious agreement on questions of
value, *gesellschaft* employs contracts, laws, and a powerful state to enforce them. Within the constraints of these laws, people are then
free to pursue their individual self-interest and develop their own
understanding of right, wrong, and what makes a good life.

Not all *gemeinschaft* cultures are honor cultures, but the con-
verse is generally true: honor cultures are almost exclusively collectivist in orientation—and we'll see why in the following chapter.
Solidarity, personal connection, and respect for tradition are foundational values for honor societies. The societies devote resources to
building and cementing bonds within the community. As we turn
away from honor, we naturally divert these resources toward more
individualistic goals. But as with risk aversion, one might wonder: Is
the shift away from collectivist values a bad thing? After all, life in
a *gesellschaft* society offers plenty of advantages. We have more individual freedom and greater tolerance for differences. We can pursue
the careers we wish to pursue and live where we wish to live. We
have financial and legal restraints but fewer moral constraints—or
at least we can determine our own moral constraints. Tradition can
be stifling and restrictive, whereas freedom is, well, liberating.

In fact, however, the safest and wealthiest societies are not
the happiest. Human beings are deeply social animals. For the past
150 years, sociologists have shown how feeling connected to one's
community leads to greater happiness and a reduced risk of depression. The evidence is overwhelming. Durkheim famously showed

that suicide rates were significantly higher in modern, impersonal, less integrated societies. A 2016 study of twenty-seven European countries found that people were happier and healthier in more socially cohesive societies. Each of the three domains of social cohesion—connectedness, social relations, and focus on the common good—was correlated with increases in subjective well-being. Though hard to measure, the rates of depression among tribal cultures are similarly low—and depression and suicide rates skyrocket after rapid modernization. We see a similar pattern in the military. Soldiers spend much of their lives in highly cohesive communities. After they leave the military, they show high risks of depression and post-traumatic stress disorder (PTSD). The risk comes both from the horrors they experience on the battlefield but even more from the shock of social isolation after living in the communal society of their units. (Suicide rates are no higher for veterans who faced combat than for those who did not.) According to the US Department of Veterans Affairs, between 11 percent and 20 percent of veterans deployed in Iraq or Afghanistan suffer from PTSD or severe depression. A RAND Corporation study put the number at 20 percent. For all of its advantages, our modernized, technologically advanced, individualist society has resulted in the highest rates of depression in human history.

Lack of social cohesion is also correlated with higher crime rates. Criminologist Freda Adler examined low-crime societies across the world to see what they had in common. Among the shared characteristics were "social cohesiveness, a strong family system, and social control systems which 'do not aim to control by formal restraint.'"

Individualist *gesellschaft* cultures require formal and impersonal systems of punishment to reduce crime. If you commit a crime, you undergo trial and go to prison. This might satisfy one's abstract sense of justice, but the impersonal process-oriented nature of the punishment is abysmal at reducing the rates of recidivism. Public reprimand from wrongdoing, Adler found, is particularly effective when "expressed by a social group to which the offender belongs." The more impersonal the criminal justice and law enforcement systems, the higher the crime rates.

Criminologist David Kennedy applied these insights when developing Operation Ceasefire (also known as the "Boston Miracle"), a program implemented by the Boston Police Department that produced a 63 percent reduction in youth homicide rates (people twenty-four and under), a 50 percent reduction in homicide among all age groups, and a 44 percent reduction in the rates of armed assaults. Kennedy would walk into meetings with police officers and gang members and say the following: "Show of hands, please, everybody who was really afraid of the cops growing up, please raise your hand. Room of a hundred cops, three, four, five will [raise their hands]. Show of hands, please, everybody who was really afraid of your mother, please raise your hand. Every hand goes up. My hand goes up, the AV guy's hand goes up, the people replacing the coffee raise their hands. 'I'm still afraid of my mother,'" somebody will say." For Kennedy, this simple anecdote says "everything you need to know about informal social control," he concludes. "Communities have tools law enforcement can but dream of."

Bottom line: communal ties are necessary for flourishing, well-functioning societies. We ignore this insight at our peril. The breakdown of communities in so many Western cities has led to more crime and in America mass incarceration. Informal social control can work only in communities in which people know each other and care about their reputations, how they are perceived within the group. These are precisely the conditions that honor can bring out. When we reject honor, we become more like the isolated, scared, selfish individuals that philosophers like Hobbes imagined us to be.

Home of the Shameless

Finally, let's talk about one aspect of our honorless society that is widely recognized as a serious cost: the decrease in personal accountability. Consider, for example, the famous case of Ethan Couch. As polarized as Americans are these days, everyone came together to denounce the sentencing of this teenager, or more precisely the reasoning behind the sentence. To refresh your memory: The sixteen-year-old was speeding, very drunk, through a residential area. He lost control and crashed into a group of pedestrians. Four people died. One person in Couch's truck was paralyzed. For all of this, Couch received a sentence of ten years' probation and a stint in a cushy rehab clinic. At the time of the crash, Couch had a blood alcohol content three times the legal limit. During the trial, the defense team brought in psychologist Dick Miller, who testified that Couch suffered from "affluenza." Affluenza, he explained, was a diminished capacity to connect actions with consequences because of a privileged upbringing and permissive parents. Couch had too much freedom as a young child and was never punished for bad behavior. Because of Couch's condition, Miller claimed, he could not be held accountable for the behavior that led to the four deaths.

Miller's testimony and the judge's sentence caused such unanimous condemnation because of what it symbolized: the vanishing sense of personal accountability that was so evident in the wake of the 2008 financial crisis. An irony lurks behind all the outrage, though. Whereas the term *affluenza* likely deserves whatever mockery it gets, the diagnosis is totally consistent with widely accepted legal and philosophical ideas about responsibility, ideas that have deep connections to the rise of individualism in the West. The focus on individual freedom has led philosophers and legal theories to place a robust "control condition" on responsibility, roughly the principle that we cannot be accountable for anything that is beyond our control. To be responsible in the modern sense, individuals must understand the consequences of their actions, intend to perform them, and be in a position to know whether the act is right or wrong. Couch certainly did not intend to kill anyone or hurt anyone. True, he made the choice to drink and drive. But the reasoning behind the control condition makes it entirely plausible to ask how much control a spoiled teenager with parents who never punish him had over the decision to drive drunk. Indeed, as I've argued in my early work, when you take the control condition to its logical extreme, the result is that no one is morally responsible for their actions. Why? Because our actions are the product of our heredity and environment, and ultimately we have no control over either.

The strict association of responsibility with control might seem so intuitive as to be self-evident. But in fact, as I mentioned in the prologue, it is a culturally local and historically recent development, confined mostly to the WEIRD (Western, educated, industrial, rich, and democratic) people of the world. My book *Relative Justice* demonstrated widespread differences in attitudes about when it's appropriate to blame and punish people. Much of the variation that I found was in honor cultures. Whereas honor cultures make distinctions between intended and unintended actions, they typically don't see control as the whole story when it comes to responsibility. Indeed, many regard it as shameful to make excuses by appealing to a lack of control. In honor cultures, taking responsibility is a bedrock moral principle. Consider a familiar case, already discussed—the NHL. Hockey's honor code is fundamentally about personal accountability. The word appears sixty-three times in Ross Bernstein's book on the subject. "We learned the code as kids up in Canada," says former player Glen Sonmor. "They were our rules for how we were going to conduct ourselves above and beyond the official rules of what the officials would enforce. It was a marvelous system based on honor and accountability." "When I grew up on a farm in Canada with six brothers," says Marty McSorley, "we had to answer for what we did. That made us pretty tough, no question. There was no running back to Mommy when things didn't go our way, so we had to stand up for ourselves and be accountable. Respect was earned in my family; it wasn't just given to any of us."

Or think back to the case of Georg, the Albanian highlander from Kadare's novel, discussed in Chapter One. Georg's grandfather did everything right after the stranger's arrival. He gave him food and shelter and walked him to the outskirts of the village. Yet because a sniper happened to be right at the town's border and because the body happened to fall at a certain angle, the grandfather was deemed responsible and had to make amends. Two generations later, Georg, who had not participated in the feud himself, was held to account after his brother was killed. It's not that Georg and his grandfather were unaware that they had no control over the events. It's that they don't believe that their lack of control absolves them from responsibility.

Many philosophers see this as irrational, immoral, and unfair. How can we be responsible for things that are just bad luck? The WEIRD control requirement allows us to be judged only by what we can control, not for the accidents of fate. Poor Oedipus Rex took every step he could to avoid fulfilling the prophecy that he would kill his father and marry his mother. But through a series of accidents, he ends up doing both. Oedipus had no way of knowing that these two people were his parents. He had no intention of committing parricide and incest and every intention to do the opposite. Yet when he discovers what happened, he doesn't make excuses—he doesn't let himself off the hook. He blinds himself and wanders away from his kingdom in shame. How fair is that?

Perhaps, like the philosophers, you find Oedipus's attitude to be irrational or even pathological. But let's not overlook the moral advantages of this way of thinking either. There's an admirable quality to Oedipus's refusal to absolve himself—especially when compared to the modern temptation to search for every possible excuse for our conduct, to constantly let ourselves off the hook. Milan Kundera's great novel *The Unbearable Lightness of Being* is in part about how pernicious this self-exonerating mindset can be. The novel's protagonist, Tomas, sees that many of his fellow Czech countrymen who had collaborated with the Soviet regime feel no guilt, no sense of responsibility, simply because they had no knowledge of the atrocities they committed. He compares them unfavorably to Oedipus. Kundera writes, "When Tomas heard Communists shouting in defense of their inner purity, he said to himself, 'as a result of your "not knowing," this country has lost its freedom, lost it for centuries, perhaps, and you shout that you feel no guilt? How can you stand the sight of what you've done? How is it that you aren't horrified? Have you no eyes to see? If you had eyes, you would have to put them out and wander away from Thebes.'" Tomas (and Kundera too, almost certainly) finds it appalling that the Czechs would exonerate themselves simply because they did not know that it was wrong to support the communist regime. It may be true that they were unaware of the extent of the atrocities, but, according to Tomas, this is no excuse. They should feel deep shame for what they did to their own country. Tomas doesn't see Oedipus's perspective as irrational or pathological. He sees it as morally superior to that of his countrymen.

Our focus on control as a condition for responsibility, in other words, inevitably leads to a culture of excuses and ever-increasing shamelessness. Anthropologist Dan Fessler asked focus groups of eighty Indonesians from the Bengkulu Province to come up with the fifty-two most commonly discussed emotions and then rank them according to their frequency in society. He did the same for a focus group in Southern California. Shame was second for the Indonesians but forty-ninth (!) for the Californians—well behind "bored," "frustrated," "offended," and "disgusted." Shame, of course, has deep connections with honor. Indeed, many anthropologists refer to honor cultures as shame cultures or "honor/shame cultures."

Shame's disappearance from our emotional vocabulary has had plenty of harmful effects. To this day, virtually no one in the financial industry has taken responsibility for their role in the 2008 banking crisis that sent the economy into near depression. The precise causal factors behind the crisis are complex and controversial, but one thing is certain: it was fueled by greed and shamelessness. And that shamelessness persisted long after the collapse. Senior executives at banks bailed out by the government still received bonuses in the millions. When the public expressed their outrage, the executives complained that they were being singled out, vilified, all part of a cynical attempt to generate "class warfare." Honor cultures probably rely too much on shame, but our modern alternative is an epidemic of shamelessness. If we incorporate a contained form of honor back into our moral experience, we can find a balance that encourages personal responsibility without leaving us all at the mercy of luck, oracles, and fate.

Shamelessness, rampant individualism, a cowardly aversion to risk—these are complex phenomena, and the factors that have produced them are complex too. Now, I don't want to overstate the case. Turning away from honor has been one contributing factor, but there are plenty of others. The sheer size of Western nations, the diversity of their citizens, and the commitment to free-market economic principles have all played a role. The good news is that we can push back against these unfortunate modern developments fundamentally transforming societal structures. And honor can help.

In the remaining chapters, I'll outline many of the specific mechanisms that honor frameworks offer for building a more courageous, cohesive, and accountable society. I'll begin with the issue of community. As we've seen above, our commitment to individualism has come at a price. Social cohesion leads to happier and less selfish people, safer and more cooperative communities, and resilience in the face of danger and hardship. Unfortunately, society is headed in the opposite direction. Is this movement inevitable, a necessary result of modernization and population growth? Or is there a way to recapture the sense of community without losing the freedom to define ourselves and our conception of a good life? And how does honor fit into this picture? In the next chapter, I'll offer some hopeful answers to these questions, exploring the deep connections between honor and solidarity.

CHAPTER 3

HONOR AND COMMUNITY

This is our fucking city.

—DAVID ORTIZ, BIG PAPI

I love Boston. I love the people, the neighborhoods, the accent. I love novels and movies set in Boston. And most of all, I love Boston sports. After the Red Sox lost to the Yankees in 2003 because of a mind-bogglingly indefensible managerial decision, I couldn't speak for two weeks. About a month later, I went out to dinner with my dad and stepmother and was thrown out of the restaurant after getting into a fight with a Yankees fan at the bar. (I was thirty-three years old.) I believe there should be a new circle of hell for the corrupt, sniveling weasel Roger Goodell and all the National Football League owners for inventing the scandal known as "Deflategate"— the physics-defying, *ressentiment*-driven fantasy that led to Tom

Brady's suspension and the Patriots losing a first-round pick. I love that people hate Boston fans for still complaining even at the most successful time in Boston sports history.

It's not just me. Bostonians in general have a proud, angry, passionate relationship to their professional teams. It's like living in a turbulent marriage. Yes, we've had unprecedented success lately, but it hasn't always been that way. Even in the bad times, though, underneath all the bitterness and coaching grievances, Boston fans show love and devotion like no other city in America. For some athletes, the relationship can get a little intense. But the ones who stick around tend to appreciate it and feel closer to the city as a result. And nothing brought that connection out like the Boston Marathon bombing in 2013.

It was on Patriots Day, one of the best holidays of the year for Boston kids. The rest of the country's students have to go to school, while Boston kids get an 11:00 a.m. Red Sox game and the running of the Boston Marathon. On this Patriots Day, though, two Chechen brothers with pressure-cooker bombs in their backpacks turned a glorious day into one of chaos and tragedy. The brothers set off their bombs about twelve seconds apart near the crowded finish line of the Marathon. The explosions caused three deaths and hundreds of injuries, including at least fourteen people who required amputations. Immediately following the attacks, first responders, race volunteers, medical staff, bystanders, and runners rushed to the aid of the injured people to help them get to nearby hospitals as soon as possible. All of them showed tremendous poise and courage, charging into a potentially dangerous area, not knowing whether another bomb would explode as they were helping the victims. The two brothers fled the scene of the crime.

Two days into the subsequent manhunt, the brothers struck again, murdering a Massachusetts Institute of Technology police officer and then carjacking a Mercedes from a Chinese immigrant. The car's GPS led law enforcement to nearby Watertown. The older brother, Tamerlan Tsarnaev, was killed in a gunfight, but the younger brother, Dzhokhar Tsarnaev, escaped in the confusion. With one of the killers still at large, the police issued a "shelter in place" order (essentially a lockdown) for Watertown and surrounding areas. Public transit systems in Boston were suspended. Schools were closed. Streets were deserted. Not since the Watts Riots had an urban area been shut down on this scale.

If the story ended here, it would be just another example of society's unhealthy attitude toward risk. This young man had committed a horrific crime, but as a columnist for the *Harvard Crimson* put it a year later, "It was us who gave the brothers two days of public fear and cowering of the kind that two sadistic thugs might envision, hope for, and relish." But the story doesn't end there. The next night Mayor Thomas Menino lifted the order, and the second brother was found hiding in a boat, injured and unarmed. And the following day, the Red Sox played their first game at Fenway Park since the morning of the bombing.

Just before the game, the wildly popular team leader, David Ortiz, known to all of Boston as "Big Papi," grabbed the microphone to speak to the sellout crowd. "All right Boston," Papi said. "This jersey that we wear today, it doesn't say Red Sox. It says Boston. We want to thank you, Mayor Menino, Governor Patrick, and the whole police department, for the great job they did this past week. *This is our fuckin' city*, and nobody's gonna dictate our freedom. Stay strong."

The crowd went crazy. The speech hit exactly the right tone, colorful language and all. Even the comically puritanical Federal Communications Commission recognized its importance. Its chairman, Julius Genachowski, tweeted: "David Ortiz spoke from the heart at today's Red Sox game. I stand with Papi and the people of Boston."

Why was Papi's speech so special? Because it appealed to the honor of the Boston people. *"This jersey...doesn't say Red Sox. It says Boston."* Papi reminded Bostonians that they were a tight community. The bombings were not an attack on the dignity of all human beings; they were an attack on the city of Boston. And Boston would bear the primary responsibility of taking care of its own.

"Nobody's gonna dictate our freedom." The speech also had a hint of rebuke. No longer would fear from terrorism keep people in their homes or restrict their liberty in any way. No more citywide lockdowns and curfews for possibly armed nineteen-year-olds, no matter what they had done.

Originally a hashtag on Twitter, the phrase *Boston Strong* became a sustained movement. Over the next year, local charities raised more than $60 million to help the victims. Boston bands like Aerosmith and the Dropkick Murphys played benefits to raise more money. Many of the sports teams biggest stars visited amputees in the hospitals and worked out with them during their rehab. The athletes worked with communities and raised money for victims and their families. And to cap it off, despite the inevitable fear of copycat crimes or further terrorist plots, the 2014 Boston Marathon saw a record turnout of runners. Many ran their first marathons with sponsors to raise money for the injured victims and their families.

As I write this, four years have passed, and people are still studying Boston Strong and holding it as a model for how communities can come together in the face of terrorist threats. In 2016, after a terrorist attack in Belgium, President Obama called Boston's response to the bombings "one of my most powerful memories and one of my proudest moments as president.... [T]hat is the kind of resilience and the kind of strength that we have to continually show in the face of these terrorists."

The Harvard Kennedy School and the Program on Crisis Leadership produced a white paper called "*Why* Was Boston Strong?" that analyzed the strengths of Boston's response. They summarized their findings as follows:

+ A part of Boston Strong is *pride* in the inspired work of those involved in responding to the event—the bystanders, the other runners, the Boston Athletic Association volunteers, the first responders, the medical staff at the finish line, the doctors and nurses and support staff in the hospitals, police from all responding agencies, fire, National Guard; in short, everyone who helped. From their dedicated, selfless work springs inspiration.

+ Another part of Boston Strong is an expression of *resilience*—that people, including those directly and indirectly injured, those involved in the response, and the community as a whole, will come back, stronger than ever, going on with their lives and hopes and dreams.

✦ And a part of Boston Strong is an expression of *unwillingness to be intimidated*. This is a forward-looking form of resilience—the community refuses to cower, to be deterred or diverted from its ongoing work and life and hopes and dreams.

Pride, resilience, and an unwillingness to be intimidated—three of the most central values in honor cultures across the world. In essence, the Kennedy School report identified honor as the source of Boston's strength.

Boston is far from an isolated case. Research shows that in general, community solidarity offers enormous benefits for people coping with tragic events. In one study, James Hawdon and colleagues analyzed three cases of mass shootings—one in Omaha and two in Finland—and examined the effects of solidarity on well-being. They measured solidarity by asking participants to indicate how much they agree (on a five-point Likert scale) with six statements:

1. I am proud to be a member of my community.
2. I feel I am part of the community.
3. People in my neighborhood share the same values.
4. My neighborhood is a good place to live.
5. I trust my neighbors.
6. People work together to get things done for this community.

The authors found in all cases that solidarity was significantly correlated with greater well-being and a reduction in the incidence of depressive symptoms.

By examining these six measures of solidarity, we can begin to see why honor-oriented values are more effective for building solidarity. The morality of dignity doesn't encourage us to take pride in our community unless the community is all of the human race. Indeed, to identify too closely with one's community is inconsistent with dignity if it leads us to exclude out-group members from our primary sphere of moral concern. Dignity also has no interest in neighbors sharing the same values. A basic tenet of Western liberalism is that people should be free to form their own values, as long as they don't violate the rights of others. Honor value systems, on the other hand, embrace each of these elements and therefore offer significant psychological benefits for people dealing with tragedy.

Moreover, it's no coincidence that honor norms emphasize this sense of togetherness. Although solidarity is valuable for all communities, it has special importance for communities in the environments in which honor norms tend to emerge. To see why, we can turn, somewhat ironically, to the groundbreaking *Culture of Honor*, by cultural psychologists Richard Nisbett and Dov Cohen. (It's ironic because Nisbett and Cohen don't talk about solidarity much at all in their book; they focus on why people in honor cultures might have a propensity for violence. But bear with me.) Nisbett and Cohen famously hypothesized that the higher rates of argument-related homicides in the American Southeast are in large part a product of the honor-oriented cultural heritage of its settlers. Whereas the northern states were mostly settled by farmers, the southeastern states were settled by Scotch-Irish herders who came from regions that weren't suited for agriculture. Anthropologists

have documented that herding societies across the world have much
higher rates of violence than farming societies.

Why is that? Well, farming communities and herding communities have different ecological and social environments, and different
norms and attitudes emerge to adapt to the particular challenges of
each environment. Herders lead precarious lives. Their livelihood
depends on protecting their livestock and areas for grazing, so they
continually face the possibility of losing their entire wealth from a
raid. And raids from opposing groups are common because they are
so profitable when successful. In addition, herding societies tend to
be in low-population, low-density areas that are not conducive to
law enforcement. Consequently, families typically have little or no
dependable protection from the state. All of these features, according to Nisbett and Cohen, made it essential for herdsmen to develop aggressive public reputations, to deter other groups that might
be considering a raid. The norms of herding communities should
therefore emphasize honor values like courage, aggression, concern
for reputation, as well as a disposition for violence in response to insults. (Insults, as you'll recall from Chapter One, can often be a way
to probe for weakness.)

Nisbett and Cohen's theory is justly famous, well supported by
subsequent research, and it reignited research on honor across dis-
ciplines. I certainly would not be writing this book if it were not for
Culture of Honor. One unfortunate consequence of honor's reputation, however, is that people too often associate it *exclusively* with
violent propensities and a heightened sensitivity to insult. This gives

a misleading or, at best, a woefully incomplete picture of honor as a whole. Part of the problem is that the environments of the particular honor culture they were studying—American Southeasterners—have radically changed. Southerners in the present no longer belong to herding communities—indeed, many don't belong to any specific community—and so Nisbett and Cohen were forced to conduct their investigation on individuals rather than groups. Their methodology entailed conclusions that could shed light only on individual character traits. The data could not reveal anything about the characteristics of honor *groups*. However, the same theory that helped to generate their hypothesis about individuals also predicts that honor groups would have a strong collectivist orientation.

For consideration, while it's true that herding groups need individuals who are willing and able to use violence for protection, it's even more important for individuals to fight not just for themselves but also for the good of their group. A herding group filled with selfish individuals would be sitting ducks for more cohesive out-groups to exploit. And remember, herding environments lacked a reliable system of law enforcement, so group members needed to count on one another that much more for protection. As Nisbett and Cohen note, herders have been the best soldiers for centuries, and good soldiers are known for their communal spirit at least as much as for their violent tendencies. It's natural, then, that strong communal norms would emerge to foster these ties, binding the members of the group together with shared values and a common purpose. Farming communities, on the other hand, could much better afford a more individualistic orientation. Since raids were less profitable and much less frequent, each individual family could focus on themselves and their crops.

Thus far, we've seen the benefits of solidarity in general and why it has special value for honor communities. For the remainder of the chapter, I'll discuss the many ways in which honor helps to create and sustain communal ties. In doing so, I'll focus on two broad features of honor: the emphasis on group identity and the distinctive approach to conflict and competition.

Honor and Group Identity

Perhaps the starkest difference between moralities of honor and dignity lies in their perspective on group identity. Dignity is a thoroughly cosmopolitan value and is therefore skeptical of narrow forms of identification (for example, with one's nation, class, family, culture, or race). The reason for the skepticism, as I noted earlier, is that when we identify too closely with our particular group, we risk excluding outsiders from our sphere of moral concern. Honor takes pretty much the opposite view. In most honor cultures, giving equal weight to group interests and the interests of strangers is thought to be immoral. You can treat out-group members with respect and generosity, but taking care of your own is a central moral priority. If this seems selfish or arbitrary, consider that many people who join honor groups are marginalized and vulnerable. Take gangs, for example. Writer Jeff Chang chronicled the rise of street gangs in the 1960s and '70s in the Bronx, a turbulent time, to say the least, for the borough's residents. Gangs served to structure the chaos. Chang writes:

> For immigrant latchkey kids, foster children outside the system, girls running away from abusive environments, and thousands of others, the gangs provided shelter, comfort, and protection. They channeled energies and provided enemies. They warded off boredom and gave meaning to the hours. They turned the wasteland into a playground. They felt like a family. "We like to ride and we like to stay together so we all do the same things and we're happy that way," said Tata, a Savage Skull girl. "That's the only way we can survive out here, because if we all go our own ways, one by one, we're gone."

For otherwise isolated individuals, joining a gang offers a sense of community as well as, crucially, protection from outside threats. As I was revising this chapter, I came across a documentary called *Check It*, about the only known gay and transgender gang in America. The Check It gang originated in Washington, DC, with just a few members who decided that forming a gang was their only hope for survival. As its reputation grew, so did the numbers. As one man puts it in the movie, "In many impoverished areas, just being black, you have a lot of odds against you. Being gay and black? It's a nightmare waiting to happen." These young men and women have been kicked out of their homes, ridiculed by teachers, bullied relentlessly in school and on the streets. Check It gives them an identity and a means of getting respect.

"It's like a family I always wanted," says one member, "and when we go out, we go out as one." Like all urban gangs, Check It adheres to a code of honor, and that can lead to violence. If you mess with one of them, you mess with all of them. They fight for each other whenever one of their members gets hassled or harassed. Over several years they built a reputation for using aggression in response to disrespect. That reputation allows them to dress how they like and go to public places without being harassed. "If no one is going to stand up for us," says another Check It member in the film, "we'll stand up for ourselves."

Honor critics might point out that if everyone adhered to the principles of dignity, the rights of these people would be respected and they wouldn't need to join gangs to protect themselves. That may be true, but the Check It members live in the real world, not an ideal one. The sad truth is that the individual liberty that dignity champions is a luxury afforded to a small portion of relatively privileged people. Banding together and adhering to gang codes is often the only means for marginalized and vulnerable individuals to get the respect they need to navigate their world. Moreover, even an idealized dignity society can contain isolated and desperately lonely people who yearn for a community, a family they always wanted. If the violence and aggression of gangs like Check It could be contained, then the gangs would be worth preserving just for this feeling of collective concern.

But as we know all too well, collective concern is a scarce resource in large free-market democracies. Healthy forms of group identification must be cultivated and fortified. Honor cultures have a lot to teach us on this front. They have practices, rituals, initiation ceremonies—both formal and informal—to build this strong sense of togetherness. Navy SEALs, for example, put their soldiers through grueling boot camps and training regimens, and they make officers and enlisted men train side by side. "We're all in it together," writes former SEAL Marcus Luttrell, "and the first thing they instill in you at INDOC (the 3 week 'indoctrination' course) is that you will live and train as a class, as a team.... Teamwork. They slam that word at you every other minute. Teamwork. Teamwork." This technique of team building traces back to the Spartans, where even the king would endure the same punishing physical training as the rest of the army.

Collective identification also creates a sense of collective responsibility that further strengthens the bonds within the group. One of the four core principles of the SEAL honor code is to "take responsibility for your actions and the actions of your teammates." The code commits them never to abandon a man, dead or alive, on the battlefield. These bonds are possible only with a powerful egalitarian and collective ethos that's at the heart of honor. In many honor cultures, when one individual violates a norm or doesn't meet expectations, other group members feel shame—real shame; they share responsibility for the act. This baffles many of us in individualistic dignity cultures. In my book *Relative Justice*, I described the reactions of Korean Americans to the shootings at Virginia Tech by Korean student Seung-Hui Cho, who killed thirty-two people in all. A reverend and founder of the Oriental Mission Church in Koreatown released this statement: "All Koreans in South Korea— as well as here—must bow their heads and apologize to the people

of America." And South Korean ambassador Lee Tae-sik called on
Korean Americans not just to be ashamed but to repent as well. He
suggested a thirty-two-day fast, one day for each victim of the car-
nage. A reporter from the NPR program *Day to Day* sought reactions from the Korean community in Los Angeles but had a hard
time finding anyone who agreed to be interviewed. When a local
real estate agent finally agreed to be interviewed, he expressed deep
shame about the killings. "But you had nothing to do with it!" the
reporter said incredulously. The man replied, "I know, but he was a
fellow Korean." In a country with such a deep commitment to individualist ideals, this attitude made no sense whatsoever.

In addition, honor's emphasis on reputation is crucial for building a cohesive and responsible community. "Your reputation begins
right here," Luttrell recalls his boot-camp instructor telling his unit.
"And so does the reputation of Class Two-two-six. And that's a reflection on me. It's a responsibility I take very personally. Because
reputation is everything." Far from being inherently selfish (as some
believe), concern for reputation is in fact a cornerstone of many
contemporary theories of human cooperation. In tight-knit social
groups, people who value reputation are more likely to perform
costly or risky cooperative behavior, especially in public settings.
From an evolutionary perspective, the benefits of high reputation
can offset the costs and possible risk of cooperating (by providing,
for example, greater access to potential mates). The more we value
esteem from others, the more incentive we have to try to earn that
esteem. When we don't care what people think about us, the incentives for costly cooperative behavior diminish accordingly. And

thanks to the principle of collective responsibility in honor cultures, the concern for reputation extends to the group. If you act shamefully, you don't just sully your own reputation; you sully the reputation of the group. On the flip side, when you act virtuously or heroically, the group benefits and feels its share of pride.

Another way that honor cultures sustain a sense of group identity is to have external marks of membership—such as jackets, uniforms, tattoos, or gang colors. "Back in England every family had their coat of arms," says a former member of the Bronx gang Savage Skulls. "This is our family coat of arms.... This is what we are; this is what we be. You give me respect. I give you respect. Simple." Even something as simple as a fan's team jersey can mark you as part of a group. You might think it's silly for grown men and women to wear the jerseys or T-shirts of their favorite team. But these items have a genuine function. I can go to a sports bar in most US cities and have an instant connection with people who would otherwise be strangers.

Many critics of honor find it utterly irrational to identify with something like a sports team. Ryan Brown, for example, gives this comically melodramatic account of a visit to an Alabama doctor just before a big college football game between Alabama and Oklahoma, where Brown resides. The physician's assistant told Brown that he wanted Alabama to beat the Oklahoma Sooners badly: "After all," he explained, "I've got to recruit against them next year." Brown reflects on the episode:

> As my body was wracked by an involuntary dry heave, I marveled
> over this man's degree of personal identification with his favorite

college football team. He was going to have to recruit against my team—against every team—for the next football season. He was a physician's assistant, not a sports recruiter. This delusion went deep, and this man needed to be handled with care, as do all full-throttled partisans in a culture of honor.... You can never be sure how far such a man might go to assert his supremacy when his honor is on the line, and this man had access to needles, drugs, and things that can make incisions.

Now, obviously, this physician's assistant knew very well that he didn't literally recruit football players for Alabama. There's no delusion at all, never mind a deep one. Brown paints a simple use of *we* in connection to the team (something virtually all sports fan do) as some sort of dangerous hallucination. This mindset is sadly all too common among academics, and it's one that we should reject wholeheartedly. Identifying with your teams is not just fun, but one of few remaining ways to connect with strangers of different races, classes, and backgrounds. We should work to preserve these opportunities for personal connection whenever we can.

Speaking of sports, let's now turn to another way that honor groups build solidarity: through competition and conflict.

Competition and Conflict

Many believe that conflicts can only divide communities, but the truth is closer to the opposite. Take feuds, for example. Honor cultures are notorious for their feuds, and there's no denying that they can cause tremendous suffering and unnecessary loss of life. But feuds also foster a deep sense of social harmony and cohesion within the feuding groups. Indeed, some anthropologists regard this to be the primary evolutionary function of tribal feuds, the reason they've persisted, even with the loss of life that they cause. When you think about it, it makes sense that feuds would bind communities together rather than tear them apart. As we saw earlier with the Boston bombing, greater solidarity naturally emerges under conditions of adversity, risk, and threat. The ever-present possibility of violent feuds in some cultures creates near-constant adversity, so it's not surprising that greater solidarity would result.

In many cases, of course, the costs of feuding in suffering and death outweigh the benefits of greater solidarity. In more contained environments, however, feuds can strengthen social bonds without subjecting communities to excessive danger. I hate to keep going back to this, but the clearest example again is sports. Whether it's the Olympics or professional or school athletics, competition breeds a communal spirit among teammates and fans. And unlike blood feuds or gang wars, sports have a built-in form of containment. You risk losing games, not lives. The stakes are still plenty high. A big game can *feel* like it's life or death, especially at the highest levels of competition. But it remains a feeling, a metaphor, not the reality.

In team sports, players depend on each other to accomplish goals they've spent a big part of their lives pursuing. Opponents are obstacles to those goals, and teams love to rally around a common enemy. Great rivalries lead to closer bonds among teammates and a greater connection with the team's fan base. In some sports, coaches and players will invent beefs or start fights solely as a means of ce-menting bonds within the team. In hockey, writes Ross Bernstein, an *individual* fight is often about respect or revenge, but the team brawl "is all about building team unity and male bonding.... It is a tremendous show of solidarity when guys know that they can count on each other in battle." Professional athletes often say that the hardest thing about retiring is the sudden absence of the communal spirit they experienced while they were playing. Like military veter-ans, they often have a hard time adjusting to the more individualis-tic way of life in the greater society.

The benefits of solidarity in athletics are present at all levels of competition. For both males and females, participating in high school team sports leads to more community engagement and a greater sense of self-respect. High school and middle school athletes report significantly higher rates of "social capital," which denotes the networks and the relationships that help children negotiate their paths into adulthood. School athletes feel greater support from their teachers and families and experience lower rates of depression. The benefits are even stronger for female athletes than for males. High school can be a lonely and isolating place for anyone; sports are one area where students can establish connections with the larger community.

Coaches and managers in team sports often cultivate an "us against the world" attitude to reinforce the team bonds. As we know, adversity bolsters solidarity, so coaches may create conditions of ad-versity even when they don't exist. Patriots head coach Bill Belichick takes this strategy to comical extremes, getting players to believe that the entire sports world doubts their ability even when they're heavy favorites to win the game. The strategy works in other domains too. Michael Feinberg, cofounder of the KIPP charter school program that serves children from disadvantaged backgrounds, gives what he calls a "locker-room speech" to the students at KIPP schools. He quotes alarming statistics, tells the kids that a lot of people out there are convinced they're going to fail, that they won't graduate, go to college, or get a degree. But if they come together and help each other, he tells them, they can prove these people wrong. The Prison Entrepreneurial Program that I mentioned in Chapter One employs a similar strategy in its classes with prisoners. It quotes the high recidivism rates and the difficulty for felons to get jobs. The goal is not to alarm them, of course, but to unite the prisoners around a common purpose, a shared struggle they'll face as a group.

These strategies fit beautifully within a larger honor framework. But a dignity framework? Not so much. Dignity can't support "us against the world" because it sees no division between "us" and the "world." Dignity's slogan is "We are the world"—which sounds nice in principle but can be isolating in practice. Individuals can truly belong to a family, sports team, gang, class, or school group. But the "human family"? It's difficult, maybe impossible, to feel connected to something as massive as all of humanity except in the most abstract and metaphorical manner.

To this point, I've been discussing the social benefits of conflicts between competing groups. No less important for strengthening communal ties are internal or *within-group* conflicts. Nineteenth-century sociologist Georg Simmel regarded conflicts as an integrating force that offers "inner satisfaction, distraction, relief" and gives "'vitality and reciprocity' to relations we might otherwise avoid." Conflict, according to Robert Nye, quoted in Simmel, not only preserves social relations but "is one of the concrete functions which actually constitute it." In other words, internal conflicts do more than just strengthen or revitalize the bonds within a group. They are a *part* of solidarity. Conflict is one of the materials out of which social relations are constructed. If this sounds counterintuitive, consider a more concrete example. Think of the closest married couple you know or the closest family. Are they the ones with the fewest arguments and conflicts? Probably not. Too much agreement and aversion to conflict are often signs of emotional distance and a deadening of relations. (Interestingly, John Stuart Mill expressed a parallel thought about opinions. Without the presence of conflicting opinions, our own beliefs become dead dogma. Even when our beliefs are true, conflicting opinions are crucial for giving us "the clearer perception and livelier impression of truth, produced by its collision with error.")

The great Norwegian criminologist Nils Christie offers a similar diagnosis in a more contemporary context. He argues that modern industrialized societies suffer from too little conflict. The paucity of conflicts, he argues, reflects the depersonalization of social life. Christie regards the sharp reduction of defamation cases—crimes against honor—as a dangerous development. The absence of defamation, according to Christie, doesn't show that honor has become more respected, but rather demonstrates that "there is less honor to respect." In a large anonymous society, everyone lives in their own corner, their own bubble. Honor conflicts are one of the few remaining opportunities for people to connect outside of their bubbles. With "less honor to respect," people have no grounds for conflict and can retreat to their own comfortable segment of society.

One of the profound insights of the restorative justice movement is that conflicts provide opportunities for social engagement and active group participation. Modern nonhonor cultures largely shun these opportunities. We marshal out our conflicts to specialists, lawyers, and judges who have no personal connection to the case or the people involved. (Indeed, legal officials can be disqualified for having such a connection.) Christie sees the modern justice system—a cornerstone of dignity cultures—as "one of the many cases of lost opportunities for involving citizens in tasks that are of immediate importance to them." Honor cultures, by contrast, have more conflicts and typically don't rely on outside forms of resolution. Consequently, they learn to become peacemakers themselves and develop a variety of rituals and ceremonies that allow people to hash out their differences face-to-face. Anthropologist Jared Diamond, for example, describes a compensation ceremony in a New Guinean tribe after the accidental killing of a child by a man from a neighboring village. The "dead child's family and the child's accidental killers, previously strangers to each other, sit down and cry together and share a meal a few days after the death." In the United States, as Diamond observes, the child's family "would be planning a civil lawsuit and the accidental killer's family would be consulting lawyers and their insurance broker to prepare to defend themselves against the lawsuit and possible criminal charges." Our legal proceedings do more to drive people apart than bring them together.

Conflict-resolution rituals offer benefits for the surrounding community as well. The Japanese, for example, often hold two ceremonies following every crime. The first is a kind of shaming ceremony, designed to reinforce the norms the offender violated and to encourage the offender to apologize and offer restitution to the victim. Then, after the sentence has been served, they have a ceremony of repentance and reacceptance. As John Braithwaite, one of the architects of the restorative justice movement, puts it, "The moral order derives a very special kind of credibility when even he who has breached it openly comes out and affirms the evil of the breach." Nils Christie, himself an inspirational figure in restorative justice circles, takes this idea even further. Conflicts, he observes, are opportunities for "norm clarification." Not just clarification in the sense that Braithwaite proposes—a reaffirmation of previously determined values—but also in the sense of discovery. Conflicts can illuminate the presence of norms that were previously unknown, unarticulated, or even undetermined. Resolution rituals allow communities to explore normative commitments and expectations in a lively, active way.

Some readers might complain that I'm cherry-picking examples—highlighting only the warm, fuzzy side of honor-related conflicts and resolutions. What about gang wars and endless beefs? Or how about duels? Haven't we done well to move beyond that practice? Isn't it obvious that duels over honor were a divisive (not to mention bloody) force within society and not a unifying one?

Actually, no. Historical and sociological research suggests that duels have a bit of a bad rap. The practice in fact offered many social benefits. In particular, duels served to maintain the egalitarian codes of an honor group. Indeed, early opponents of the duel, such as Francis Bacon and Cardinal Richelieu, opposed it on precisely these grounds. Bacon wanted to expand the power of the monarchy and further distinguish ranks among gentlemen. The equalizing function of duels was an obstacle to the kind of hierarchy he wanted to create. Duels were also much safer than commonly supposed. Dueling rituals were designed to testify to the honor of the combatants while at the same time minimizing the risk of death or injury. The combatants would use "inaccurate and weak smoothbore pistols" or swords that were "modified to prevent deep penetrating injuries." Many challenges were resolved without fighting of any sort, as "the mere willingness of both parties to show up for the fight was often satisfactory." The point of the duel was more "to demonstrate one's status-group membership than to establish dominance over one's opponent. Thus it was less important to win than to display courage."

Although the time of the duel has long passed, there are modern parallels that reflect the duel's egalitarian ethos. Former National Basketball Association (NBA) player Steve Kerr recalls an incident with his superstar teammate Michael Jordon, a notorious bully during practices. During one practice, Jordan talked his usual trash to Kerr, and Kerr snapped back at him. In response, Jordan "punched him in the face right there on the court." As Kerr remembers it now, "It was one of the best things that ever happened for me. I needed to stand up and go back at him, I think I earned some respect. But we have a great relationship ever since.... [Y]ou gotta prove it and then once you prove it, you're fine."

Or consider the fighting rituals of many poor urban neighbor-hoods. In *The Code of the Street*, Elijah Anderson describes several fights involving a black fifteen-year-old young man named Tyree in Philadelphia. After moving to a new neighborhood, Tyree gets beaten up by a gang of "bols" (slang for friends) in public and suf-fers a serious loss of respect as a result. As with the duels, beatings like this have a ritualized form of constraint—though it's much less formalized. The goal is to test someone for weakness, but "not to hurt him physically to the point where blood is spilled and he might have to go to the hospital." Still, Tyree has to respond to reclaim his self-respect and the respect of the neighborhood kids. So he tells his grandmother not to call the police. He cleans himself up and goes back to the store to find one of the bols who beat him up. When he finds one, he walks up and punches him in the face. He gets a few good punches in and then stops immediately once the bol's nose starts to bleed. Tyree shows ritualized restraint of his own, doing just enough to get his respect back and no more. After another more formalized fight with a stronger member of the group, the bols wel-come Tyree into their circle—to their honor group.

Anderson also describes a third fight that helps to cement a friendship. After some time Tyree develops a bond with a boy named Malik. They watch each other's backs in other neighbor-hoods and start to bond like "brothers" or "cousins." But one day Tyree senses that Malik is disrespecting him in front of a group of girls. He tells Malik he's sick of getting dissed and challenges him to a fight. As Anderson describes it, such fights "are part of a long and honorable tradition of settling disputes between men." They are characterized by elaborate rules, including "no hitting in the face," "you got to use just your hands," and "no double-teaming." (After an accidental slap, Tyree apologizes profusely before getting back to the fight.) The fight lasts about twenty minutes, with no clear winner. Anderson writes:

> They have fought, and, for the moment, settled their differences. But, actually, something much more profound has occurred as well. To be sure, the two boys can now smile at each other again, knowing that if they have a disagreement, they can settle it man to man. Through this little fight, they have bonded socially. They have tested each other's mettle, discerned important limits, and gained an abiding sense of what each one will "take" from the other. With this in mind they adjust their behavior in each other's presence, giving the other his "props," or respect.... [I]n effect, they learn the rules of their relationship.

Like duels, what seems like a violent conflict is in fact a way of resolving a dispute and equalizing the parties. Winning or losing doesn't matter; they just have to show heart. Recall too Christie's idea that conflicts are opportunities for norm clarification. For Tyree and Malik, the fight helped them learn the rules, the norms, of their friendship. And yes, on some occasions, these rituals go badly wrong and someone gets seriously hurt or killed. But that just speaks to the need for containment. When the rituals function properly, they lead to greater social cohesion and a more equal status for all parties.

Equality, incidentally, is itself highly correlated with greater solidarity and higher rates of civic participation. One of the worst misconceptions about honor societies is that they are essentially hierarchical. On the contrary, honor cultures tend to be far more egalitarian in practice than dignity cultures. The egalitarian spirit is necessary to build cohesion, collective responsibility, and group loyalty.

In theory, of course, the morality of dignity supports egalitarianism as well. But the size, diversity, and impersonal nature of dignity cultures tend to produce tremendous income and status inequality and a corresponding reduction in solidarity.

It's true that the honor codes of neighborhoods like Tyree's emerge in conditions of scarcity and adversity and that the codes have their downside, especially for young men who don't have Tyree's toughness. We should therefore be on the lookout for other more contained forms of conflict—such as athletics or restorative justice—that bring similar gains in solidarity without as many of the burdens.

This chapter has examined the psychological benefits of group solidarity and explored some of the ways that honor works to strengthen it. I've argued that honor can help to mitigate the isolating effects of modernization and that we should therefore try to cultivate it to bolster the collective spirit of our communities. You might think that I've painted too rosy a picture of the group dynamics of honor cultures. What about the political polarization? Or the demonization of out-groups? The nationalism? The tribalism?

And not everyone in impoverished urban communities settles their beefs like Malik and Tyree. People bring guns to fistfights and get shot in drive-by shootings. Gang-related homicides in some cities like Chicago are at an all-time high. The honor codes that call for settling beefs yourself can lead to violent multigenerational feuds. What good is solidarity if you're dead? All good questions. In the next chapter, I'll try to answer them.

CHAPTER 4

VIOLENCE AND AGGRESSION

Norms of aggression have evolved in honor cultures to adapt to the challenges of their environment, and consequently honor cultures are typically more violent than dignity cultures. But the moral of this story is complicated. Excessive aversion to violence has produced ineffective zero-tolerance policies, the school-to-prison pipeline, a massive police state, and the largest prison system in human history. Moreover, honor-based violence helps us resist oppression and maintain self-respect in the face of dehumanizing forces. The pros of honor-based violence can far outweigh the cons, especially when the violence can be properly contained.

Why Are Honor Cultures More Aggressive?

Imagine you're a college student who has agreed to be a subject in a psychological study. The experimenters tell you to fill out a demographic questionnaire and then turn it in at a table at the end of a narrow hallway. You fill out the form and start walking down the hall-way, and then a tall grad student walks out of a door marked "Photo Lab." He opens a big file cabinet that blocks the hallway. When he sees you, he closes the file drawer to let you pass. You turn in the form and start to head back down the same hallway to the experi-ment room. The grad student sees you again, slams the file drawer shut, bumps you in the shoulder, and says, "Asshole." Before you can react, the student heads back into the door marked "Photo Lab."

How would you feel if that happened to you? The answer may depend on where you're from. In their famous experiment, Michi-gan psychologists Richard Nisbett and Dov Cohen (mentioned in the previous chapter) hypothesized that students from the south-ern "honor" regions of the United States would take the insult more personally. They would be angrier and in a more violent state of mind. And that's exactly what they found. In one study, neutral observers who didn't know the students rated the southerners' re-action as "angry" and the northern students' reaction as "irritated" or "amused." Southern students also had greater increases in cortisone levels (a hormone related to stress) and testosterone than the north-ern students in the insult condition. In the control condition with no insult, the hormone levels were the same for both southern and northern students. Last, all students read written scenarios after the insult that featured ambiguous offenses—like a driver cutting off another driver on a road. Southern students were more likely than northern students to predict that the scenario would end violently. These emotional and physiological differences in the two groups of students were especially striking given that the southerners were college students from relatively wealthy families attending the University of Michigan. Although they came from regions associated with honor, you might expect the effects on their behavior and physiology to diminish with their exposure to the norms of college life in the North.

In another well-known experiment, Nisbett and Cohen sent a series of fake cover letters to employers across the country. The applicant in the letter explained that he had been convicted of felony manslaughter and wished to clarify what happened, in hopes that the employer would still consider his application. He came from a small town, he explained. One night he was having a drink in a local bar, and an acquaintance started boasting that he had slept with the applicant's fiancée. The man laughed in his face and told him to step outside if he was man enough. So they went outside and fought ("I was young, and I didn't want to back down from a challenge in front of everyone"), and the other man was killed—unintentionally. As Nisbett and Cohen predicted, southern employers were more compliant than northern ones, more likely to offer contact information or job applications, and more likely to offer sympathy in their responses. One southern employer, for example, wrote back to say that although she had no openings at that time, the incident was not a problem for her. "Anyone could probably be in the situation you were in," she wrote. "It was just an unfortunate incident that shouldn't be held against you. Your honesty shows you are sincere." There were no comparable expressions of sympathy from the North.

These studies and many others, Nisbett and Cohen argued, help to explain the higher rates of argument-related homicides in the

American Southeast. In cities with populations of fewer than two hundred thousand, the rates among white males for non-argument-related homicides were roughly the same in the northern and southern cities. But the rates for *argument-related* homicide were twice as high in the South. In the larger populations, southern cities had significantly lower rates of non-argument-related homicides than those in the North, but again had much higher rates for argument-related crimes. The increases, according to Nisbett and Cohen, were a product of honor norms favoring violent retaliation in response to personal insults and challenges.

What's behind the connection between honor and this particular brand of violence? Why do people in honor cultures have such different behavioral, emotional, and physiological reactions to insults? I discussed this question briefly in the previous chapter, but it's worth returning to Nisbett and Cohen's account in more detail. The authors proposed that norms and dispositions for violence tend to emerge under specific ecological and social conditions typically found in herding or pastoral societies. Some features of these environments include the following:

1. Less cooperation between strangers and fewer anonymous interactions period. The cooperation that occurs in these societies is primarily within tight-knit groups and among kin.
2. Precarious wealth and livelihood. Protecting resources is crucial for survival, and raids or thefts can destroy the wealth of an entire family or group.

3. Little or no reliable protection from the state. The societies tended to be relatively lawless in comparison with industrialized or agricultural communities.

Norms of aggression and a higher sensitivity to insult have vital functions in environments with these features. Since the benefits of thefts are higher, people have more incentive to use insults as a probe for weakness. Failure to respond to insults or challenges makes you a more attractive mark for a theft or a raid. If you develop a reputation for weakness, you'll signal to potential thieves that you're incapable of defending your animals. If, on the other hand, you develop a reputation as a hair-trigger retaliator, outraged at the slightest provocation, offenders are far less likely to take advantage of you. It's not worth the risk. Having a violent reputation is like having a guard dog. When burglars see the dog, they'll move on to the next house, the one without the dog. Of course, developing a violent reputation carries risks of its own, but they're outweighed by the prospect of losing your property, wealth, and livelihood in a single raid.

In honor cultures, emotions and norms work together to make people more inclined to act violently in response to insults. The southerners in the "asshole" experiment were angrier and more stressed than the northerners. And they were more likely to endorse norms for violent behavior in the written scenarios. According to the best evolutionary models, cultural norms evolve within societies to adapt to the demands of the environment. Cultures tend to have norms that help them cooperate, survive, and reproduce in the part of the world in which they live. But people don't think of norms in such pragmatic terms. Once norms get entrenched, we observe them for their own sake, not merely for their instrumental value. If you're in an honor culture, you'll believe that backing down from a challenge is cowardly, that standing up for yourself is simply the right thing to do. Emotions reinforce these convictions. After backing down, you'll actually feel greater shame than someone from a nonhonor culture.

There is plenty of social pressure to conform to these aggressive norms too. In the Corsican honor culture, people who don't avenge offenses are "the target of the whisperings of his relatives and the insults of strangers, who reproach him publicly for his cowardice." A man who doesn't punish the person who deceives his daughter "can no longer appear in public. Nobody speaks to him; he has to remain silent." Among the Albanian highlanders, "A man slow to kill his enemy was thought 'disgraced' and was described as 'low class' and 'bad.'... [H]e risked finding that other men had contemptuously come to sleep with his wife, his daughter could not marry into a 'good' family." The Japanese warrior culture of Bushido compels cowards to commit ritual suicide. "Death before dishonor" is a common proverb across many honor societies.

Men are usually the ones who perform the violence in honor cultures, but women are central to transmitting and reinforcing the norms of violent behavior in the face of challenges or insults. Women vigilantly hold the men to account and make sure they don't back down out of cowardice. As William Ian Miller writes, the women in honor cultures understand that "man is more naturally chicken than wolf." They devote massive cultural resources to motivating acts of revenge to overcome this resistance and remember past wrongs. "People," Miller writes, "especially the women in those cultures, would not let you forget, though sometimes they might let you forgive when prudence not only was a sensible policy but could be made to look like an honorable one too." In ancient Greece, women performed mourning rituals after a killing to inflame the men's passions for retaliation. The maidens of Sparta sang songs of ridicule to humiliate anyone who displayed cowardice on the battlefield. When a Spartan warrior accused of being a "trembler" returned to the city, "the pretty young girls clustered around him, mocking him and defaming him with these anthems of shame." And if they ran to their mothers? A Spartan mom would lift up her skirt to her son and say: "Where are you running—back here from whence you came?" In many impoverished urban neighborhoods, mothers, fathers, brothers, and sisters believe they must drill messages like "Don't punk out" and "Respect yourself" to their children for their own protection. Mothers and fathers sometimes punish children for not being sufficiently aggressive. If a child loses a fight, a parent might respond, "Don't come in here crying that somebody beat you up; you better get back out there and whup his ass. I didn't raise no punks. If you don't whup his ass, I'll whup yo' ass when you come home."

So the norms for aggression in honor cultures are reinforced on every level, through the community, the family, and an individual's emotions and hormone levels. Consequently, honor norms can be "sticky"—meaning that they don't necessarily change when the environment around them changes. Most southerners these days aren't herders, with their entire livelihood at risk from a single theft or raid. They aren't oppressed; they don't live in a lawless society. Nevertheless, they continue to abide by the traditional norms of hospitality, politeness, and violence in response to insult.

So far, I've given you the descriptive story, an explanation of the connection between honor and violence. But the morality of these norms for aggression is an open question. Most of us don't live in pastoral environments. Most of us don't have livelihoods that depend on developing a violent reputation. Does this suggest that we would do better to rid ourselves of honor values and the violent norms that typically come with them? In the remainder of this chapter, I'll argue that the answer is a qualified no.

Is Violence Immoral?

Ethicists tend to equate violence with moral wrongness as a default, and it's easy to see why. Violence causes harm and suffering. Therefore, violence is wrong. Since honor often promotes and even celebrates acts of violence, we should reject honor as immoral as well. But matters are not so simple, morally speaking. Suppose Pinker is right that the "civilizing process," the transformation from honor cultures to dignity cultures, has led to a decline of violence. We can't evaluate the decline in isolation—lower rates of violence have moral costs that must be factored in as well. Large nonviolent societies require a powerful state and a massive law enforcement apparatus.

They need Leviathans at every level—schools, workplaces, national and local communities—and the Leviathans come with a steep moral downside. Take, for example, the zero-tolerance policies in schools that were put in place to eliminate school violence like fighting and bullying. Yes, they produced a reduction of school violence, but they've also led to a proliferation of student suspensions and created a school-to-prison pipeline for low-income students. Meanwhile, the ever-increasing public demand to keep violent criminals off the street has produced a deeply unfair prison system and the highest prison population in human history. One of the great self-serving myths in the United States is that if we just eliminated prison sentences for low-level drug crimes, we would get our prison population under control. In reality, drug sentences are responsible for 16 percent of prisoners in state prisons, and only 5–6 percent of that group are both low level and nonviolent. The explosion of the US prison population is the result of prosecutors responding to panic about the violent crime wave in the 1970s and '80s. True reform requires that we shorten or eliminate sentences for violent criminals, something even the best-intentioned people seem reluctant to do.

So that's one complication to the story: the moral costs of eliminating violence from society. Here's another: most acts of violence are morally motivated. This is what Alan Fiske and Tage Rai argue in their excellent 2015 book, *Virtuous Violence*. Of course, Fiske and Rai are anthropologists; they're not making ethical judgments about the violence. Their thesis is purely descriptive: people who act violently are usually driven by moral motives rather than selfish ones. According to Fiske and Rai, morality is about regulating relationships, and human beings employ four basic frameworks for regulating their relationships. The first involves acting within a community. The second involves acting within a hierarchy. The third involves issues of fairness and equality. And the fourth involves proportionality and market exchange. The motives for violent behavior, they argue, almost always come out of these four frameworks for regulating relationships.

Of course, "morally motivated" doesn't mean "morally correct." According to Fiske and Rai's account, even something as abhorrent as honor killings counts as morally motivated. Families rarely want to kill a daughter, sister, or cousin suspected of having extramarital sex. But they feel obligated to restore their honor within the community; they feel it's their moral duty. So for Fiske and Rai, it counts as morally motivated. (And the same goes for most gang violence, corporal punishment of children, and even many cases of rape.) From our perspective, honor killings are plainly immoral, ethically off-the-table, whether they are motivated by moral considerations or not. For many other cases of honor-related violence, however, it's helpful to understand the motives behind the behavior in order to properly evaluate it.

Consider, for example, a famous recent case of honor-related violence: Zinedine Zidane's head butt in the 2006 World Cup final, an act that led to a red card and his ejection in the final game of his career. Again, I'll turn to my running foil, social psychologist and honor scold Ryan Brown. Brown uses this case as an example of the pathology that comes from embracing an "honor ideology." Here is Brown's account of Zidane's action:

From most people, a head-butt to the chest would not amount to much, but from Zidane it was a stunner, knocking Materazzi to the ground. What provoked the assault that led to Zidane being ejected from the game? Was it a racial slur, as many speculated in the days that followed? Did Materazzi call Zidane a terrorist or something equally obnoxious? No and no. It turns out, Materazzi insulted Zidane's sister. For someone like Zidane, steeped in the honor culture of his parents' homeland of Algeria, such an insult is greater than a racial slur, and it cannot be ignored—even if not ignoring it means getting ejected from the final game of the World Cup, and the last game of your career. Even if it means your team loses that final game (which they did). Stained honor must be cleansed. Asked about whether he would be willing to apologize to Materazzi almost four years later, Zidane's response was classic honor syndrome: "Never. It would be to dishonor me....I'd rather die."

For Brown, it's obvious that Zidane acted wrongly. France ended up losing the match, and Zidane's ejection might have cost them a World Cup. And many commentators following the incident agreed, writing that Zidane was selfish to retaliate in that manner. He let down the country, they wrote, all because he couldn't shrug off a childish insult to his family. But calling the act "selfish" is clearly a mistake. Zidane didn't benefit from his ejection. The last thing he wanted was to get ejected from the World Cup final, the final game of his career, knowing that his team had to play a man down, at a distinct disadvantage. What Zidane faced was a moral dilemma, with conflicting duties from within the community framework. Zidane had a duty to help France's team win the championship. But he also had a duty to defend the honor of his sister—to make his family proud, to make his hometown proud.

Many people recognized the complexity of the incident. In fact, in the days following the incident, much of the condemnation focused on Materazzi, who had baited Zidane the whole match, insulting his family and calling his sister a whore. In an interview on the French television station Canal Plus, Zidane apologized for getting ejected but said he didn't regret doing what he did. He had shrugged off many of the Italian's insults throughout the match, but the dam broke when he insulted Zidane's family: "I would rather have taken a punch in the jaw than have heard that." Indeed, it was *Materazzi* who apologized for the incident, not Zidane, and he made sure to clarify which member of Zidane's family he had insulted. "What annoyed me most," Materazzi said later in an interview, "was that some supporters or journalists said that I insulted his mother. I would never have allowed myself to offend his mother, because I lost mine a long time ago."

Opinion on Zidane was split in Europe and in the United States, but not in the Marseille urban ghetto where Zidane grew up. They loved it. To them, Zidane's head butt was a source of pride, not shame. Insults to family members can't just be let go, even if it hurts your team's chances of winning the World Cup. Further interviews revealed just how much the act was rooted in Zidane's ties to his community. "It's hard to explain," Zidane said, "but I have a need to play intensely every day, to fight every match hard. And this desire never to stop fighting is something else I learnt in the place where I grew up. And, for me, the most important thing is that I still know who I am. Every day I think about where I come from and I am still proud to be who I am: first, a Kabyle [a Berber region of Algeria] from La Castellane, then an Algerian from Marseille, and then a Frenchman."

The pride was reciprocated. An Algerian sculptor created a fifteen-foot bronze sculpture of the incident. (The sculpture was placed in the Centre Pompidou museum in Paris, indicating that the French fans were not on board with the sanctimonious condemnation of many commentators.) And Zidane's mother told a British newspaper, "Our whole family is deeply saddened that Zidane's career should end with a red card but at least he has his honor. Some things are bigger than football."

Now, I'm not saying that Zidane clearly did the right thing, although I lean in that direction. The point is that evaluating the act requires taking many factors into account: Zidane's character, his pride, his toughness, and his loyalty to his family, hometown, heritage. You have to consider the whole moral package. And look: Materazzi wasn't seriously hurt, and the act didn't lead to a long-running feud; at worst, it cost France a World Cup. It's a tough moral call, because there were strong moral considerations on both sides.

Maybe you don't find this case as tough as I do. Well, then, consider a context where honorable violence is not just morally motivated but also morally commendable—more virtuous than nonviolent alternatives. Living under conditions of oppression, for example. Dignity doesn't have much to recommend for the oppressed.

Dignity is passive; it tells us to respect others and not to violate their rights. Okay, but how should we respond when our rights are violated? On that question, dignity is silent, and honor has a lot to say. Honor says, "You should be prepared to fight and even to die to preserve your self-respect and the respect of others in your group."

It's no accident, then, that oppressed groups often appeal to honor rather than dignity to battle oppression and fight for respect from the larger society. In her book *Liberalism with Honor*, political theorist Sharon Krause offers many examples, including this moving account of how Frederick Douglass used honor to conquer his own sense of himself as a slave. The turning point for Douglass was an act of resistance against a vicious master named Covey. One day, after a brutal beating, Douglass resolved to defend and protect himself the next time Covey attacked him. Krause quotes from Douglass's autobiography:

> I now forgot my roots, and remembered my pledge to *stand up in my own defense....* Whence came the daring spirit necessary to grapple with a man who, eight and forty hours before, could, with his slightest words have made me tremble like a leaf in a storm, I do not know; at any rate, *I resolved to fight*, and what was better still, I was actually hard at it. The fighting madness had come upon me, and I found my strong fingers firmly attached to the throat of my cowardly tormentor; as heedless of consequences, at the moment, as though we stood equals before the law.... The cowardly tyrant asked if I "meant to persist in my resistances." I told him "I *did mean to resist, come what might.*"

After two hours, Covey gave up the contest, huffing and puffing. Trying to rescue his own dignity, Covey said, "Now you scoundrel, go to your work; I would not have whipped you half so much as I have had you not resisted." But as Douglass writes, "The fact was, *he had not whipped me at all*."

Douglass regarded his act of violent resistance as a watershed moment: "It rekindled in my breast the smoldering embers of liberty...and revived a sense of my own manhood." Fighting back allowed him to reclaim his honor, Krause says, "in the sense that it made him respectable in his own eyes and in the eyes of 'human nature' itself." Human nature, writes Douglass, "is so constituted that it cannot *honor* a helpless man, although it can *pity* him."

After slaves were freed in the United States, honor continued to motivate African Americans in their struggle for equality. At the outset of the twentieth century, W. E. B. DuBois called on black Americans to "sacrifice money, reputation, and life itself on the altar of right...to reconsecrate ourselves, our honor, and our property to the final emancipation of the race for whose freedom John Brown died." Even Martin Luther King Jr., the civil rights leader most associated with nonviolent resistance, expressed the same opposition to gradualism and the same readiness to die for his cause. "As much as I deplore violence," he wrote, "there is one evil that is worse than violence, and that's cowardice." King went further: "No man is free if he fears death."

Another group who turned to honor in response to persecution are the Jews of eastern Europe in the nineteenth and early twentieth centuries. Jews at that time and place were subject to continual maltreatment, forced to live in filthy ghettos, separate from the rest of society. They were denied economic opportunities and access to culture, legal redress, and basic human services. According to legal scholar Orit Kamir, pre-Zionist rabbinic Jews conceptualized these abuses as a kind of cosmic trial, a purifying punishment from the heavens. They saw themselves as victims and martyrs, suffering for the glory of God. The founder of Zionism, Theodor Herzl, on the other hand, denounced this attitude. He declared it passive, submissive, cowardly, and feminine. He reformulated Jewish oppression as a national humiliation, a disgrace to Jewish honor. Honor doesn't encourage seeing yourself as a victim and leaving it at that. Honor regards being victimized as shameful and motivates you to restore your wounded pride.

Once Herzl embraced this logic, one of his first actions was to challenge a leading anti-Semite to a public duel. He would either live and restore Jewish honor or die and show that Jews were as brave as anyone else—that they preferred death to dishonor and disrespect. Herzl rejected incremental solutions like gradual settlement in Palestine: Rather, "Jews were to think big, to practice bold and risky self-assertion, to seek sweeping solutions that would alter their situation in one fell swoop." They would proclaim these aims to the world no matter what the risk to the fragile Jewish infrastructure in Ottoman Palestine. And they would rid themselves of their "blighted physiognomy." They would nurture physical courage with rewards of medals and prizes for those who displayed it. Herzl, in other words, used all the tools of honor—shame, pride, public recognition, rewards, and medals—to strengthen resolve among an oppressed people to fight back against the persecutors.

In addition, as we've seen in previous chapters, honor encourages collective identification, which is a crucial component of group resistance. For this reason, many black leaders in the United States have long been suspicious of so-called respectability politics. To Black Power leaders like Stokely Carmichael and Charles Hamilton, respectability politics means rejecting your identity as a black person and striving to become "white." Black people who do this "are required to denounce—overtly or covertly—their black race, they are reinforcing racism in this country." Carmichael and Hamilton reject the morality of dignity's focus on the individual, stripped of his or her group affiliation. In their view, the power of oppressed groups derives from what it could do as a collective. The nature of oppression makes it difficult to combat alone. By dividing the group into individual atomic units, you drain the power of a movement's resistance.

Herzl understood this too when he conceptualized the persecution of Jews in eastern Europe as humiliating and dishonorable for *all* Jews. This connection can cross national borders, enlisting anyone who identifies with the group to help the cause. In my interview with honor scholar William Ian Miller, he told me a good story about the famous Jewish gangster Bugsy Siegel. Siegel was approached by fund-raisers for the Haganah, a Jewish paramilitary organization, in the early twentieth century: "And Bugsy," Miller says, "he don't know from nothing about the Haganah. So they explain to

him who they are and say, 'We need guns. We need weapons.' And
Bugsy says, 'You mean Jews are killing people?' They say, 'Well, yeah,
we have to; we're fighting.' Bugsy says, 'Jews are killing people?' And
he writes them a check."

With Herzl, there seems to have been an element of calculation
in his decision to reject the idea of persecution as "heavenly purifi-
cation." More often, honor norms and values emerge naturally and
get integrated because of their effectiveness. The norms shape emotional dispositions and are shaped by them in turn. A "fighting madness" came over Douglass when he refused to back down against the
cruel slave owner. But then Douglass recognized the importance of
his honorable resistance and embraced a norm for this kind of behavior. It then became a guiding norm for Douglass as he formed a
resistance movement.

Under conditions of oppression, then, violent honor norms can
be moral goods, providing the clearest—and at times the only—path
to collective resistance, self-respect, and the respect of the oppres-
sors. In recent times, people have also turned to violence to combat
the alienating effects of inequality and modernization. The past few
decades have seen the rise of backyard bare-knuckled brawling, fight
clubs, and other forms of illegal "sport fighting"—a response to the
highly rationalized controlling forces of the modern state. Fighting,
according to the participants, provides a way for them to get respect
that's absent in their jobs and their daily experience. When they
fight, they feel in control, however temporarily, over their destinies.
Academics in particular have trouble understanding this perspective.
Philosophers may not have high salaries, but we get tremendous

autonomy, a relatively high degree of control over our day-to-day affairs, compared to other professions. Most people, especially people in poverty, don't have that autonomy and turn to violence as a form of liberation. "Fighting is the ticket, brother," explains an underground fighter. "When I step in that cage nothing is holding me back.... I can let go of everything pent-up inside that I have no control of. I like having the power.... My whole life has been dictated for me, where I go to school, what sports I play, how I live." Another fighter, only eighteen years old, says: "I've got school on Tuesday, Wednesday, and Thursdays. After school I work, and on my days off I work, or I study, or I see my family. Sometimes I feel that my entire day is full of things others have told me to do." Although these people aren't battling organized forms of oppression, they nevertheless see honorable (and largely contained) violence as a form of liberation and control in a society that doesn't respect them.

But now let's consider another case, one that may be harder to square with the idea of virtuous violence—bar fights among the white working class in the South. Sociologist Heath Copes has studied the attitudes and values of white men living in and outside Lafayette, Louisiana. He and his colleagues interviewed men between the ages of twenty-two and forty-eight who had been in multiple fights as adults, including at least one fight in the past three months. They found that the men typically operated according to a shared code of acceptable violence. The code was imbued with significant meaning "as a reflection of inner integrity and honor." They thought of themselves as "peaceful warriors" who didn't seek out violent confrontations but didn't back down from them either.

It's an honor code through and through: stand up to aggression, never take insults lying down, prove that you're not a coward. The code calls for loyalty, expressed through acts of courage. One interviewee named Kevin puts it like this: "It's important to show who you are as a man, how you feel about yourself, and how you feel about your friends and loved ones, that you're there to protect them. People, even your friends, need to know that you're there for them… that you have the strength to stand up for yourself and kinda prove you're a man." Emotions like pride, shame, and guilt—all tied to the ideal of manhood—function to enforce the code. When asked how he would feel if he didn't fight after being insulted, Kevin answered, "I'd feel guilty. I'd feel weak. I'd feel like I let myself down. I'd feel like I let anybody else that was involved down." Another man, David, said: "I hate to use the word, but the word pussy comes to mind…. That you punked out and you couldn't handle your own business." A third man, Eric, answered: "That I just wasn't a man, straight and simple. I feel like if I'm tested and I walk away, if I didn't fight that person or prove myself, you know, I'd just feel real down on myself and feel like I'm kind of a coward. There ain't nothin' more that I hate than feelin' like a coward. So, if I'm tested, I'm gonna do what I gotta do to not feel like a coward."

Critics of honor often point to attitudes like these as examples of "toxic masculinity," a pathology that causes men to try to expose weakness and dominate the people around them. But the code of these Lafayette southerners doesn't encourage domination, just active resistance to the domination of others. They distinguished themselves from "agro dudes that have something to prove and go out looking for trouble." In fact, they didn't even consider themselves to be violent. They were peaceful warriors, not "thugs" and "violent people." A man named Renee explained: "Guys that work out and they just go out to the bars with their tight shirts that show their muscles, and they get drunk, and they go out, they lookin' for a fight. That's why they go out that night. You can tell when you see 'em. You know they lookin' for something. That's the type of people that I think are like street people, thugs, you know. I consider them violent people." The code, in other words, imposes constraints on violent behavior. All the interviewees strongly condemned those men who used violence for robberies and other crimes or who fought just to demonstrate violent prowess. The code promotes fighting only for legitimate reasons.

The Lafayette men did express concern for their reputations and their roles in the social hierarchy. But the concern with hierarchy was more defensive than ambitious. Multiple respondents, according to Copes et al., "made reference to primitive man or the animal kingdom to show that physical confrontation and dominance contests are natural." They believed that the self-respect that comes from defending yourself physically "will expand and trickle through all aspects of your life." Otherwise, "you would be equal to a sitting duck. The same way sharks smell blood and animals smell fear. People see fear and capitalize on it. You know big fish, little fish kind of thing." Fighting was a way of establishing their place in the natural pecking order. The goal wasn't to rise to the top, but simply to maintain a respectable position within the social order. Most participants, according to Copes and his colleagues, placed themselves in the middle range of fighting ability and said they weren't particularly tough guys.

Like many honor codes of ritualized violence, the Lafayette code regarded fights as far more likely to defuse violent conflicts than to prolong them. The fights, according to participants, often functioned to settle bad blood and prevent resentments from lingering. Copes et al. write: "Fighting also was perceived as cathartic. Adversaries can release the stress of tense situations with a flurry of punches. After the violence, emotions settle. Even on the losing side of the fight, these men accepted that they could resolve conflicts with violence and that it could prevent lasting conflict. Indeed, most believed that dangerous animosity was unlikely to last beyond the incident. In their circles, fights happen, and in most cases, people get over them." Even the losers of fights would share this perspective. One of them, Cain, explained that "if you're the person who starts it and you end up getting your ass handed to you, you get what you deserve. You feel stupid you know, but you know you had it comin'."

The code has a blend of pragmatic and principled aspects. The men believed that standing up to challenges is virtuous and honorable in and of itself. But they also recognized the practical value of fighting as a deterrent. If you don't fight when insulted, said Fred, "you're laying the foundation to get beat up again, picked on, taken advantage of, or exploited later." Dana offered an example of someone who repeatedly hit on his wife: "I told him to back off, and he didn't so I knocked him out. After that he never fucked with her again.... [The police] wouldn't have solved anything. Really, I solved it. Maybe it wasn't the way everybody wants it to be handled, but it was handled. I got my point across and it never happened again." And like most honor codes, this one strongly discouraged involving the police in personal affairs. Handle your own business; don't let others fight your battles.

Overall, Copes and colleagues paint a picture of a relatively high-functioning honor code that regulates violent behavior and keeps it within reasonable boundaries. Several elements make this happen. First and foremost is the widespread agreement about the constraints for honorable violence. All the men, for example, believed it was dishonorable to try to cause serious injury in a fight. The code requires that that you give quarter once it's clear that you've won the fight and to stop fighting when opponents can no longer defend themselves. The code demands a fair fight, meaning that combatants should be roughly the same size and have equal numbers on both sides. There is no honor in fighting obviously outmatched opponents. "If you can already beat somebody up," said Eric, "it's not necessary for you to follow through with it.... [S]ome people," Eric explained, "just aren't worth beatin' up or fightin' with because I don't want to hurt 'em and I know they really don't want to fight in the first place. They're just drunk." (As an occasional drunken shit talker with no real fighting experience, my younger self benefited from the magnanimity of men like Eric on a number of occasions.)

The code also discourages the use of weapons like bottles, knives, and guns, a crucial component of limiting the costs of honor-related violence. In the middle of the twentieth century, inner-city gang violence was much like what Copes et al. describe in Lafayette, before a massive influx of guns turned some urban ghettos into war zones. When the guns arrived, homicide rates skyrocketed. Earlier I mentioned the "Boston Miracle," a law enforcement program that cut the Boston homicide rates by more than half in one year. The cornerstone of the strategy was not to prevent violence. It was to prevent gun violence. After the program was implemented, the head of Boston's gang-outreach community burst into a meeting "practically dancing," and he shouted, "I just saw a fistfight! I haven't seen a fistfight in years!"" Fistfights were the ultimate sign that the strategy was a success.

Of course, since the constraints of the Lafayette code are flexible and informal, they aren't flawlessly observed. When a friend is getting beaten up badly, the men said they might violate the "equal numbers" rule and jump in to help him. In addition, alcohol and drugs could lead to code violations that the men regretted later. Eric told the interviewer, "I beat up some guy one night just because I was intoxicated. It had nothing to do with him. It had somethin' to do with his family member. It had to do with a girl, and if I wouldn't have been in the state of mind I was in, I would've never done that to that person. He didn't deserve that." Again, this speaks to the importance of keeping guns out of the equation to avoid a literal arms race. If the constraints are occasionally violated, arming yourself and showing a willingness to shoot becomes a defensive position.

Violence Is Not a Deal Breaker

So what should we conclude? Is honor-related violence moral or immoral? I hope at the very least I've convinced you that the question, framed like that, is misguided. We can't evaluate the morality of violence in a vacuum. We have to look at the circumstances and the motives surrounding the violent behavior and frame the question in proper context. We have to understand the moral costs of policies that reduce violence—rigid school discipline and overflowing prison populations, for example. We must also recognize the virtues of violent behavior in some contexts and the important role it can play in battling oppression and preserving self-respect and a sense of control in response to dehumanizing forces. Challenges to dignity are a fact of life for almost everyone. Norms for standing up for yourself, not backing down, are important for navigating these challenges. Honor systems recognize that rhetoric about dignity and equal worth is often just that, rhetoric. In the real world, we have to take risks to earn our self-respect. This takes courage, and honor norms rightly reward courage. Finally, recall from Chapter Three that conflicts—both violent and nonviolent—are important for maintaining relationships in an increasingly segmented society. Conflicts provide opportunities for active participation and engagement with other human beings. They reconnect us with others, allowing individuals and communities to discover who they are, what they're made of, what they believe and feel. Honor-based conflict without insults leads to greater cooperation. As Nils Christie puts it, "Conflicts might kill, but too little of them might paralyze." It's impossible to completely eliminate violence without also reducing productive community-building conflict.

On the other hand, we can't be blind to the massive costs that result from the violence in the modern world either. Violent codes sometimes come with their own honorable constraints, but not always. Norms that encourage violence are hard to control, especially when deadly tools like guns are introduced into the mix. The gang wars in Chicago and other urban areas show what happens when the constraints are absent. It's essential for third-party authorities to find ways of minimizing the costs of violence—fistfights over gunfights. The same norms that promote a healthy virtuous form of courage in some contexts can lead to bloodshed and tragedy in others.

Ultimately, then, we can't deliver a decisive moral verdict on something as complex as violence. We can, however, rule out the simple syllogism "Honor values lead to more violence; therefore, honor values should be rejected." The crucial questions going forward are as follows: How much violence is acceptable given the costs of reducing it? And how can we contain the violence that exists and harness it toward virtuous ends? In the next chapter, we'll examine one virtuous end of violence: revenge.

CHAPTER 5

HONOR AND REVENGE

Honor cultures are sometimes referred to as "revenge cultures," because of their enthusiasm for the practice. Critics of honor point to this association as another reason to reject honor in favor of dignity. But revenge has many virtues, and the source of these virtues lies in the very features that moralists condemn about it: revenge is costly, revenge is risky, revenge is personal. Because of these features, the act of revenge can demonstrate personal qualities such as courage, self-respect, loyalty, and even love. Revenge has a dark side, however, and is often difficult to contain. How can we harness what's good about revenge without suffering its unacceptable costs?

"She Won't Be Smirking Soon"

My daughter Eliza's basketball team, the Mavs (the one that got a trophy after going 0–12), was truly atrocious. None of the girls could shoot, pass, handle the ball, or play any kind of team defense. Somewhere between 90 and 100 percent of their offensive possessions resulted in a turnover or a jump ball. Eliza's offensive game was even more hopeless than the others, but she took pride in her defense. The coach called her "Axe." She would hound and exasperate the girl she was guarding through sheer effort. She was our shutdown defender, usually keeping the margin of defeat within ten or fifteen points. But then came the Rockets on the schedule. The Rockets were good, and they knew how to set picks. Eliza had never played anyone who knew how to set picks. Suddenly, her best attribute, her only real way of contributing to the team, was neutralized. At halftime Eliza was close to tears in frustration after chasing their shooter around the court and repeatedly running into a girl twice her size in the process. Even worse, this team had an attitude. They were physical, they could run a fast break, and they talked trash. Their redheaded shooter, the one Eliza tried to guard, was a Steph Curry fan; she'd put two fingers to her lips and kiss the sky every time she hit a shot. That day Eliza's Mavs were beaten even worse than normal, and the Rockets crowed about it.

Eliza was crying in the car on the way home. "That girl, she was making mean faces at me…and she pinched me when I was guarding her," she told me.

"I don't know—she just had a little style. I kinda liked her," I said to her horror. "Look, they're a physical team, they weren't doing anything illegal, and if you don't want them to do that again, work on your defense and next time don't give up any easy points."

Eliza looked at me skeptically. But a seed had been planted.

As it happened, the Rockets were on the schedule the next

weekend too—back-to-back games. In the week in between, the coach taught Eliza how to set picks, and she and I worked on how to fight through them on defense. The next weekend we arrived a little late, so Eliza didn't get into the game until near the end of the first quarter. I'll now quote from an essay Eliza wrote about this game—called "Payback"—for a 100 percent accurate account of what happened next:

> I look over to the girl, the horrible girl, who seemed like the meanest person ever at that moment, and she had a little smirk on her face.
>
> *She's won't be smirking soon!*
>
> I was right. Within 20 seconds, that mean little girl was face down in the floor.

I saw it happen. As soon as Eliza checked in, the redheaded girl started streaking down the court for yet another layup. Eliza... stopped her. It was a hard foul from the sweetest, gentlest soul I know. Later in the half, Eliza went to set a pick of her own on that girl who was twice her size. She got there one half step too late and was called for a moving pick. But the girl hit the floor and Eliza stayed up on her feet. (It was a ticky-tack call too.) In the third quarter, after maybe nine minutes of playing time, Eliza fouled out—the first player to do that all year. The Mavs lost the game 32–2. On the ride home this time, Eliza had the widest grin I've ever seen.

Ah, revenge. Like so many practices associated with honor, revenge has been dismissed as irrational, selfish, and barbaric—a form of "wild justice" (in Francis Bacon's words) that has no place in a civilized society. This mentality is pervasive, even among laypeople. "I don't want revenge—I want justice" is the common and expected refrain from victims about their offenders. We *say* all this, yes, but we don't seem to believe it in our hearts. Revenge has been the most popular genre of literature, drama, and myth since Homer, and it's the most popular film genre today. We root for the avengers in these stories, and we're unsatisfied if the payback never comes. Even in cultures of dignity, people love revenge stories. In one breath, "I don't want revenge—I want justice." In another, "If there's no revenge, there's no justice."

Western moralists try to explain away our attraction to revenge as a safe outlet for our darker animal impulses. We love revenge stories, they say, because the stories allow us to indulge our primitive desires and passions without suffering the terrible consequences that these desires normally produce. But this view is inaccurate or at best incomplete. Revenge is appealing because it's an expression of human virtues like courage, loyalty, self-respect, and even love. We're attracted to revenge because other more rational, calculated, or forward-looking responses to wrongdoing often seem morally deficient in comparison. We'll begin by briefly examining these alternatives and clearing up some common misconceptions about revenge in the process. Next we'll look at three revenge stories—one from myth, one from literature and film, and one from real life—that illustrate the virtues of honorable vengeance. Finally, we'll reckon with the costs of retaliation and its potential to corrupt the honor of avengers. I'll conclude with some reflections on connections between revenge and criminal punishment, which will take us into the following chapter on justice.

Revenge Versus Retribution

Cultures of dignity are unanimous in condemning revenge but split over how to handle criminal wrongdoing. Since the Enlightenment in the seventeenth and eighteenth centuries, two opposing theories of punishment have dominated the philosophical and legal landscape: utilitarianism and retributivism. Utilitarians claim that we're justified in punishing criminals for practical reasons: criminal punishment provides benefits for society, such as crime prevention, deterrence, and rehabilitation. In the early to mid-twentieth century, the justice system operated largely according to utilitarian and rehabilitation principles. But the mood changed in the late sixties and early seventies. You can see the shift in the novels and films of that period—such as *One Flew over the Cuckoo's Nest* and *A Clockwork Orange*—dark satires of state-enforced rehabilitation of criminals. People were disturbed by the idea of criminals being rehabilitated against their will to conform with the existing norms of society; it was a disturbing vision and seemed to violate individual autonomy. You can also see the shift in vigilante thrillers like *Dirty Harry* and *Death Wish*. Ethicists couldn't extinguish that lingering feeling that people who commit crimes should be punished even when it brings no benefits for society at all, but simply because they deserve it. And so began what's known in criminological circles as the "retributivist revival," which is still with us to this day, especially in the United States.

Whereas utilitarians focus on the future, retributivists focus on the past. According to retributivists, we're justified in punishing criminals not for pragmatic or forward-looking reasons, but because they *deserve* to suffer for the immoral actions they have performed. This principle seems to capture two widespread intuitions about justice: first, that criminals should suffer for wrongdoing independent of the consequences and, second, that innocent people shouldn't be punished even if the punishment would provide benefits for society. As theorists, however, retributivists have some explaining to do. Specifically, they have to explain *why* wrongdoers deserve to suffer even when their suffering does not contribute to overall well-being. As we'll see in the next chapter, this is a difficult and maybe impossible task. The theoretical problem led to a practical one as well. Since retributivists had no satisfying account of the concept of desert (that is, deservingness), critics attacked it as an empty concept, a rhetorical disguise. Retribution, the critics said, is simply revenge dressed up to look respectable.

So now retributivists had to distance themselves and to draw a clear distinction between revenge (bad) and retribution (good). Harvard philosopher and retributivist Robert Nozick laid out five alleged differences between the two, and several are worth examining because they reflect some common misconceptions about revenge. For example, Nozick writes that retribution "sets an internal limit to the amount of punishment, according to the seriousness of the wrong, whereas revenge internally need set no limit to what is inflicted." This is a total distortion of revenge and a bizarre one at that. The plots of ancient revenge epics like the *Iliad* and tragedies like the *Oresteia* revolve around questions of the proper measure of revenge. The central concern in the honor code of the Albanian *Kanun* is to set appropriate limits for retaliation. The commonly misunderstood talionic "eye for an eye" principle from the Law of the Twelve Tables is actually a call for restraint. If you lose an eye, take no more than the other person's eye. Don't take both eyes; don't take an ear; don't kill them. Just take an eye and be on your way. Determining the appropriate boundaries of revenge is an obsession in virtually all honor cultures. And as we'll see in the following chapter, their approach to the question of proportionality is far more plausible than anything retributivists have to offer.

Another of Nozick's distinctions is largely accurate, although he takes the wrong lesson from it: "Revenge is personal," he writes, "[w]hereas the agent of retribution need have no special or personal tie to the victim of the wrong for which he exacts." Nozick is right that revenge by its nature is private and personal. And if anything, Nozick's claim about retribution isn't strong enough. It's not merely that the agent of retribution *need not* have a personal tie to the victim. The agent of retribution *should not* have a personal tie to the victim. Retribution is supposed to carry out impartial justice. Where I differ with Nozick on this distinction is that he sees it as a point in retribution's favor. I do not, but more on that in Chapter Six.

Nozick gets back to straw-manning revenge in his fourth distinction. Revenge, he claims, "involves a particular emotional tone, pleasure in the suffering of another, while retribution either need involve no emotional tone, or involves another one, namely, pleasure at justice being done." One wonders whether Nozick gets his ideas about revenge from film. Does Michael in *The Godfather* take pleasure in killing the police chief for shooting his father? Does William Muney take pleasure in killing Little Bill for torturing his friend in *Unforgiven?* Or from myth—Orestes is distraught when he avenges his father by killing his mother, Clytemnestra. Revenge *can* involve taking pleasure in the suffering of the wrongdoer. But more often it's a grim business, performed out of duty and loyalty rather than desire. Indeed, we even have a phrase for this: "the reluctant avenger." And on the flip side, although Nozick again means to praise retribution, the idea that one would take pleasure in the abstract idea of justice by inflicting suffering seems, well, creepy at best.

Having cleared up some common misconceptions about revenge, we can better evaluate it from a moral perspective. Enough philosophy—it's time for some drama. I started with a story about my daughter. Let's examine three more, all of which feature an avenging daughter of their own.

The Virtues of Revenge

Electra: Remembrance and Sacrifice

When it comes to twisted revenge stories, Quentin Tarantino has nothing on whoever dreamed up the family from the House of

Atreus. The lineage begins with King Tantalus, who decided to cook his own son as a test for the gods. His grandson Atreus topped that by chopping up, cooking, and serving all three of his nephews to their father, his brother, Thyestes. (Thyestes had slept with Atreus's wife.) Our story, though, begins with Agamemnon, Atreus's son. Drawn into the Trojan War, Agamemnon is forced to sacrifice his daughter Iphigenia to get favorable winds for his ships. After many years, he returns home in triumph. His wife, Clytemnestra, murders him in his bathtub with a little help from her lover Aegisthus: revenge for killing their daughter.

Or was it? Many characters in the story express doubts about Clytemnestra's motives for killing Agamemnon. In most versions of the myth, Clytemnestra and Agamemnon had two other children—Orestes and Electra—along with the slain Iphigenia. At the time of Agamemnon's murder, Orestes is a small boy, but the lover, Aegisthus, fears that he'll become a threat to his new kingdom later in life. Fortunately, a loyal servant saves Orestes from Aegisthus's wrath and takes the child into exile. Agamemnon's daughter Electra stays on the island with her mother and stepfather, horrified by the duplicity of her mother. She grieves loudly and publicly for her father. In Sophocles's play *Electra*—the version of the myth that I'll focus on here—Clytemnestra tries to convince Electra of her righteousness: "Tell me why he sacrificed her? Why? Was it to save the Greeks?... The dead girl, if she could speak, would take my part." But Electra doesn't buy it. "Take a close look at yourself," Electra replies. "See if you are merely offering an excuse. Tell me why, if you could, why you are committing an act beyond shame—sleeping with the murderer with whom you killed my father. And you are making children with him. But you drive out your legitimate children.... Will you argue that this too is done to pay for your daughter's death?" So Clytemnestra kicks her out of the palace and threatens to send her to live in a cave if she doesn't quit her public mourning.

After a few years, Electra decides to avenge her father by killing her mother and stepfather. But with Orestes banished, she has little hope of infiltrating the palace and performing the act. Sophocles's play begins with Electra pacing, miserable, seething with grief and rage. The chorus implores her not to waste her life in sadness and anger. Electra replies that she has no choice. "My sorrow has no natural limit," she tells them. "Come, is it natural to forget the dead? In what man is that an instinct? *I seek no honor in forgetting.*... For if he that is dead is earth and nothing. If he lies there neglected, and they pay nothing back, no death for death, then justice, shame, and piety are dead for all of mankind."

Electra fears that if she lives easy without avenging Agamemnon, it would be tantamount to forgetting him, to letting go of her father's memory. Such feelings are common in honor cultures, which see a strong connection between revenge and memory. Women often take the lead in keeping alive the memories of slain group members. Even today, women in parts of southern Greece sing "revenge lullabies" to infants and toddlers so that they will remember their murdered kin. William Ian Miller describes a ritual in the Icelandic Sagas "in which the corpse or parts of the corpse...were employed to charge a person to avenge it." In one case, a wife digs up her dead husband, chops off his head, and presents it to her uncle, who is procrastinating about avenging his brother, her husband. She tells him that the person who once belonged to the head would have already avenged him if the situation were reversed. Miller notes that the last words of the ghost of Hamlet's father in his speech urging Hamlet to avenge his death are "Remember me."

But back to Electra's story. In Sophocles's play, Electra has a sister too. Her name is Chrysothemis, and she provides a perfect contrast in personality. Like Electra, she hates her mother and especially her stepfather, Aegisthus. But Chrysothemis takes a decidedly more pragmatic approach to the situation. "Will you never learn to control your empty anger?" she says to Electra. "If I had the strength I would show them how I felt. But in this storm I must drift with lower sails. I must not seem to act and then fail. I wish you would do as I do." Electra has no patience for pragmatic thinking. She accuses her sister of cowardice and lack of integrity: "My whole life is spent seeking vengeance for my father…yet you do nothing to help. You discourage me. This is cowardice heaped on shame.… I hurt them and bring honor to the dead.… But you, *you say you hate. You say it*. But the fact is you live with your father's murderers. I would never give them the satisfaction, not if they bribed me with those gifts you revel in. Set your rich table. Live your easy life. My inner peace is food enough for me."

Electra's remark here gets to the heart of one of revenge's essential virtues. With all of its costs and risks, taking revenge shows that you're not all talk—that you truly feel the anger and grief at the loss of a loved one. It also illustrates how wrongheaded it is to think of revenge as "selfish" and how misguided it is to tell an avenger that

she won't feel any better after the deed is done. Maybe not, but it's
not about the avenger; it's about paying back a debt for the victim.
Revenge can be one of the least selfish acts imaginable, for it often requires tremendous sacrifices to bring about an outcome that
doesn't benefit the avenger in any way.

What's fascinating about the long exchanges between the two
sisters is that Chrysothemis doesn't come off as an unsympathetic or
selfish character either. She cares for Electra and is genuinely worried about her. She even takes a small risk just in coming to warn
Electra about her mother's plot to harm her. Chrysothemis isn't de-
luded either. She recognizes that Electra has the moral high ground.
She concedes that "justice is on your side, not on mine." But at a
certain point, she thinks, self-interest has to trump justice. "To die
from stupidity!" she says to Electra. "Where's the good in that?" And
it's a good question: How does it honor anyone to die for a hopeless
cause? Later in the play, Chrysothemis repeats her question. "Where
is the freedom," she says, "where is the victory and glory if we die in
shame? … There are times when even justice can bring destruction."
And so they reach a standstill. "I could not live my life on such principles," Electra replies.

The point of this story isn't to demonstrate the obvious supe-
riority of Electra's perspective, because it's not obviously superior.
Electra often comes across as hysterical, stubborn, sanctimonious,
and overwrought. All things considered, Chrysothemis may be right
to acknowledge the near-impossible odds of successful resistance.
And if the cause is futile anyway, why not indulge in a few luxu-
ries that come from being the queen's daughter? On the other hand,

given how much Electra suffers and how much of the suffering is self-imposed, there can be no doubt about her loyalty, bravery, and commitment to honoring her father's memory. Through her dedication to vengeance, Electra demonstrates genuine virtues that can't be expressed to the same degree by taking a rational, practical, self-interested stance.

If you want to know how Electra and Clytemnestra's story ends, you'll have to wait until the next chapter. For now, though, let's turn to our next virtuous avenger, a prim fourteen-year-old girl named Mattie Ross.

Mattie Ross: Revenge as an Expression of Love

Mattie is a character in Charles Portis's novel *True Grit*, which has also been adapted twice for film. At the outset of the novel, we learn that Mattie's father has been murdered: "A coward going by the name of Tom Chaney" shot and killed him while he was unarmed. Chaney then robbed her father and fled the town on his horse, afraid that he would be pursued by a group of drummers who had witnessed the murder. His fears, it turns out, were unfounded, and nobody followed him. Chaney "had mistaken the drummers for men," Mattie tells us.

So Mattie takes it upon herself to make Chaney pay for his crime. She uses what remains of her family's extra funds to travel to Little Rock and hire Rooster Cogburn, the marshal with "true grit." Having spent her money to hire Cogburn, Mattie is forced to sleep in town, in a dank, cold room, on the same bed as a snoring, wheezing, coughing old man. Soon, she becomes sick herself. Meanwhile,

a Texas Ranger named LaBoeuf arrives in town. He's also pursuing Chaney, but for a different crime—the killing of a dog and a
judge in Texas. As Mattie makes the final arrangements, LaBoeuf
offers to join up with Cogburn to track down Chaney. Much like
Chrysothemis, LaBoeuf offers a pragmatic perspective to the situation. It would be a lot cheaper for her, he explains to Mattie, if
the two joined forces, and it would improve the chances of getting
the killer. Mattie refuses, however, because LaBoeuf's involvement
would mean that Chaney would be tried for his crimes in Texas.

LaBoeuf laughs: "It's not important where he hangs, is it?"

"It is to me…," Mattie replies. "I want Chaney to pay for killing
my father and not some Texas bird dog."

LaBoeuf implores Mattie to be sensible. "He will be just as dead
that way, you see, and pay for his crimes all at once."

Mattie is not having it. "No, I do not see. That is not the way I
look at it."

Cogburn gives it a try too. "What you want is to have him
caught and punished," he tells her. "We still mean to do that!"

"I want him to know he is being punished for killing my father."

It matters to Mattie that Chaney gets punished for the crime
that's connected to her father. LaBoeuf wants Chaney hanged in
Texas so that he can get the money. Cogburn thinks it's enough for
him to be caught and punished so that justice is served. (Cogburn
is like the retributivist here, asking Mattie to be satisfied with abstract justice.) But Mattie doesn't see it that way, and she's willing to
risk her life to ensure that it doesn't happen that way. She insists on

accompanying the two men on their mission in spite of the risk to her health and safety.

Cogburn and LaBoeuf try to elude her by setting out at the crack of dawn. Mattie pursues them, at one point taking her horse into a river and almost drowning. The mission is long, hard, and dangerous. Revenge always comes with a "satisfaction not guaranteed" clause. She's almost killed several times. At the end of the novel (spoiler alert), Mattie gets her revenge, shooting Chaney herself in self-defense. But she loses her arm in the process.

Mattie's and Electra's stories have a lot in common: a slain father and a young daughter in a man's world who wants against all odds to avenge her father's death and will do whatever it takes to make it happen. Both stories have a character who represents prudence and practical reasoning (LaBoeuf, Chrysothemis) to contrast with the irrational, stubborn, costly attitudes of the heroines—although LaBoeuf is a less sympathetic, more self-interested contrast. Where the two stories differ sharply, however, are in the temperaments of their heroines. Electra wears her emotions on her sleeve, scarves, and tunics. Mattie is reserved, unsentimental, even robotic at times. (Hailee Steinfeld plays this aspect of Mattie perfectly in the more recent film adaptation by the Coen brothers.) Mattie doesn't say a single word about her love for her father, except that he was "a handsome sight" on his horse riding into town before he was shot. Yet in spite of her reserve, no one can doubt how deep the connection was between father and daughter, precisely because of what she endures to avenge his death. If Mattie had stayed in Little Rock, or if the marshal and Texas Ranger had found Chaney and brought him back to Texas, then she would have done nothing to demonstrate her love and commitment to her father. As Electra says to Chryso-themis, it is one thing to say you love someone and another thing to show it. Mattie shows it. That's what makes her a virtuous avenger.

Laura Blumenfeld: Family Pride and the Demand for Acknowledgment

I can hear you complaining now. You think I'm romanticizing re-venge, that I'm presenting an oversimplified, glorified picture of an ugly practice. I've picked two famous revenge stories in which the revenge is successfully carried out with little collateral damage, with no further cycle of violence, and in which targets of revenge clearly deserved their fate. But in real life, revenge is messy and destructive, and the question of who deserves what is ambiguous and complex.

There's some truth to this objection. I've chosen a couple of paradigm examples because they help illustrate the moral upside of a practice that many believe to be morally indefensible, entirely bad. So now I want to focus on an example from real life: Laura Blumenfeld and her revenge on the Palestinian man who shot her father. Blumenfeld, a *Washington Post* reporter, relates her account in a book called *Revenge: A Story of Hope*. It's a beautiful, inspiring memoir, and I can't begin to do it justice here. Buy her book and bump it to the top of your list. (Finish this one first, though.) Here are the CliffsNotes. In 1986 Blumenfeld's father, David, was trav-eling to Israel as a tourist. While he was there, a roving Palestinian Liberation Organization gang began gunning down people in the old city. David Blumenfeld was one of the victims, shot by a gang member named Omar. And a few years later, his daughter Laura, a quiet, diminutive Harvard graduate from a Jewish middle-class family on Long Island, embarked on a decade-long quest for revenge.

Since her father suffered no long-term injury and the shooter was in prison, Blumenfeld's obsession with revenge baffled her friends, her husband, her brother, and even her father, who was satisfied himself that justice had been carried out. (Anyone who says that revenge is only a man's game is mistaken.) Just as in the two stories above, this one features a solitary woman on a mission to avenge a wrong against her father. Everyone around the woman wants her to forget, to move on with her life, but she stubbornly persists. Blumenfeld's story even features a Chrysothemis-like character: Rachel, an economics professor at Brown University, who gently mocks Laura's obsession. Like most people in Blumenfeld's life, Rachel recommended "functional amnesia" as a response to wrongdoing. "Forgetting was the way forward," Blumenfeld writes. "I had seen this reaction in other people. Rather than take revenge, they followed the principle of maximization of expected utility: 'What happened in the past—those are sunk costs. It's all about optimizing the future. How can I maximize the present value of my future stream of net benefits.'"

But like Mattie and Electra, Blumenfeld didn't look at it that way. Maximizing expected utility can't trump her sense of family honor. This becomes explicit when Rachel asks her why she persists in this hopeless quest. Blumenfeld, almost too embarrassed to reply, makes Rachel promise not to laugh.

"I wanted them to know..."

"That you can't shoot your dad?"

"No, not that...that you can't...you can't fuck with the Blumen-felds!...That there's someone you have to answer to, and I know it's ridiculous that the someone is me."

In an interview with *Salon*, Blumenfeld elaborates on her motives. "It was about family," she says. "Revenge helps answer the question, who are you? You are what you're willing to avenge. I wanted to answer the question: Were we a family who stood up for each other or not?... It was a way of asserting our family's identity." Blumenfeld alone felt that the attack had dishonored her family and that prison was no remedy. Revenge was the only way of restoring their status as an honorable family that stood up for each other—a family that you couldn't fuck with without consequences.

So what happens? How does it end? (Major spoilers to follow.) Blumenfeld's capacity as a journalist enables her to gain access to many corners on the pretext of researching a story for a book. She meets with the shooter Omar's family many times, concealing her identity as the victim's daughter. In her first visit, she asks the father why Omar shot the tourist. The father replies that he did it for the honor of the Palestinian people, for the cause of liberation. "Anybody would do what my brother did under those circumstances," adds Omar's brother Imad. "If you pretend to be a Palestinian for five minutes, you'll feel what we feel." Blumenfeld asks Imad if he's afraid that the victim's family will take revenge. "No," he replies. "There's no revenge. My brother never met the man personally. It's not a personal issue. Nothing personal, so no revenge."

Blumenfeld hears a similar sentiment from Omar in the written correspondence she initiates with him while he's in prison. In his first few letters, it's clear that he doesn't regard the shooting as a personal wrong but rather sees it as a necessary component of an ideological struggle. Laura is disappointed. "Too much politics," she writes, "not enough humanity." This detail is common to many revenge stories. The offender sees the original wrong in an impersonal way, "just business," or as a side effect, collateral damage in service of a larger goal. The victim, in contrast, takes the act very personally. Indeed, revenge is a demand that offenders acknowledge the personal aspect of the wrong.

The story takes a complex turn. Blumenfeld develops a close relationship with Omar's family as well as with Omar himself through their correspondence. But she remains convinced in her duty to avenge her father's injury. But how? At one point, Blumenfeld's journey takes her to Iran, where she interviews the grand ayatollah. After a few general questions about the Islamic laws of retaliation and blood money, Blumenfeld asks, "What if a Palestinian shoots a Jew?" The grand ayatollah replies that Palestinians can't give blood money or be avenged because they're at war with the Jews. Blumenfeld presses further: "What if he's a tourist?" "Tourists can get blood money and revenge as long as they're not trying to occupy the Palestinian's house. They are entitled to retaliation. It's in Islamic law." The grand ayatollah, Blumenfeld writes, had granted her family the right to avenge her father's injury.

Blumenfeld finally gets her revenge at Omar's appeals trial. The trial itself is just a routine hearing over a technical issue concerning

Omar's health; a favorable verdict would probably lead to an earlier release. But when it comes to drama, the scene at the trial gives Sophocles a run for his money. Omar and his family are both present. Blumenfeld demands to speak at the trial, a request that's repeatedly denied since the judges view her as just another American journalist. Blumenfeld presses forward, and then, after more than a year of keeping her identity secret, she reveals that she's the victim's daughter. Stunned silence. Like the judges, Omar and his family were discovering the secret for the first time.

The judges ask her why she would do such a dangerous thing, referring to her undercover relationship with the family in Gaza. Blumenfeld replies, "I did it for one reason. Because I love my father very much, and I wanted them to know—he is a good man, with a good family.... I wanted them to understand, this conflict is between human beings, and not disembodied Arabs and Jews. And we're people. Not 'military targets.' We're people with families. And you can't just kill us." Blumenfeld's words express a demand for personal acknowledgment and respect. Omar is moved and understandably shaken. Blumenfeld angrily reminds him that he promised her in a letter not to hurt anyone again: "I held onto his eyes, angry, firm, hoping that he felt ashamed: 'This is on your honor,' she says. 'Between the Khatib family and the Blumenfeld family.'" The judges are impressed but have to respect the process. The two families (Blumenfeld's mother attended as well) embrace after the trial. Omar remains in prison and is released a couple of years later, after serving two-thirds of his sentence.

Some might say this sounds more like a forgiveness story than a revenge story. Blumenfeld explicitly rejects this view. At the trial, her mother stands up and shouts that she forgives Omar. "*Forgive?*" Blumenfeld writes. "Why did she use that word? This was not about forgiveness. I was not forgiving him. This was my *revenge.*" It was what she calls "revenge as transformation," which involves the demand for acknowledgment, recognition, and empathy—not destroying your enemy but "transforming him, and yourself." Omar agrees: "Laura chose a positive way of getting revenge from me. And she succeeded." And indeed, all the hallmarks of revenge are there. Blumenfeld makes sacrifices, takes risks, and demonstrates loyalty and love for her father and a strong sense of personal and family honor.

Dishonorable Revenge

In spite of what I've argued so far, I have no desire to return to the days of vigilante justice. Revenge can't function as a proper system of punishment in a large and diverse society like our own. Too often there is collateral damage, and there is a constant threat of escalation. The conflict that serves as the backdrop to Blumenfeld's story—the Palestinian and Israeli—provides so many tragic examples. One of the worst occurred on July 2, 2014, when three Israeli settlers—a twenty-nine-year-old man and two teenagers—drove through East Jerusalem looking to avenge the killing of three Israeli teenagers in the West Bank a few days earlier. A suitable target of revenge, in the settlers' minds, was someone "lightweight," whom they could quickly and easily force into their car. They came across a slightly built Palestinian named Mohammad, sixteen years old, dragged him into their Hyundai, and drove to a nearby forest. The three settlers bludgeoned Mohammad with a wrench and then set him on fire. They sped off as Mohammad burned to death. Although they tried to destroy all evidence, the three suspects were caught almost immediately. An Israeli court convicted them of murder.

As we've seen, honorable avengers demonstrate virtues like bravery, loyalty, and integrity. They take risks and accept responsibility for their actions. The three Israeli settlers showed none of these characteristics. They were cowards, looking for a physically slight victim to make the abduction easier and less risky. They had no personal ties to the Israeli victims and almost certainly knew that the victims' families would be horrified by a murder done in their names. Indeed, Rachel Frenkel, the mother of one of the Israeli victims, called the attack an outrage, "the shedding of innocent blood in defiance of all morality, of the Torah, of the foundation of the lives of our boys and all of us in the country." The killers did not accept responsibility; they tried to burn all evidence of their behavior. One of them pleaded insanity at the trial. You might say they committed the act to avenge Israel, but their fellow Israelis unequivocally condemned the act. The families of victims on both sides rejected all acts of violence in the name of their children. Former Israeli ambassador to the United States Michael B. Oren condemned the attacks, saying they "dishonor the memory of our three precious boys." If revenge is meant to honor the victim's memory, this murder did exactly the opposite.

The story highlights the central problem with vengeance: it's hard to contain, hard to get right. The passions of revenge can overwhelm the constraints that honor imposes. This shouldn't blind us to the moral advantages of revenge or to the defects of a process-oriented, impersonal justice system. But any honest account of revenge must acknowledge its deep problems too.

Dinah, Dukakis, and the Death Penalty

So what can we gather from the observations in this chapter? At the risk of trying your patience, allow me to conclude with two more quick stories that most readers will already be familiar with. The first is the story of Dinah, in book 34 of Genesis. Dinah visits the city of Shechem, where she is raped and kidnapped by the ruler's son, also named Shechem. After capturing Dinah, Shechem falls in love and wants to marry her. So the ruler goes to Jacob, Dinah's father, and asks if his son can marry Dinah. The always prudent Jacob decides to make a deal. In exchange for some land and wealth, he'll allow Shechem to marry his daughter. Dinah's brothers, though, Shimon and Levi, are still "grieved and very angry" about what happened. They say they'll agree to the deal only if all the men of Shechem are circumcised. Because his son is smitten with Dinah, the ruler agrees to the amendment. Soon, all the men of Shechem are circumcised. And three days later, "when they were in pain" (from the circumcision), Shimon and Levi enter the town and massacre everyone, including Shechem and his father.

Jacob had been unaware of this part of the plan. "What have you done?" he complains to the sons afterward. "Everyone will turn against us now! The Canaanites and the Perizzites, will try to kill us. We'll be destroyed!"

Shimon and Levi's reply concludes book 34: "Like a whore they should treat our sister?"

Along with several professors, I teach a class on the great books in the Honors College at the University of Houston. Genesis was on the syllabus one semester, and it had been a long time since I had read it. You won't be too surprised to learn that my colleagues and I reacted very differently to the Dinah story. They thought the brothers' behavior was clearly abhorrent and unjust. It's not an unreasonable view. Killing all of the males in the city for the actions of one man seems disproportionate, and convincing them to get circumcised beforehand is a macabre touch at best. On the other hand, Shimon and Levi demonstrated a virtue with this action that had been mostly absent up to that point in Genesis: family loyalty. Think about it: Cain and Abel are the first two brothers, and that ends in a fratricide. Lot offers his two virgin daughters up to be raped by a violent, horny mob. Abraham sends his wife, Sarah, to be part of an Egyptian king's harem not once but twice—all for his own protection. And then he agrees to sacrifice his only son because God asks him to. Jacob and his twin brother, Esau, started fighting in Rebecca's womb, and later Jacob swindles Esau out of his inheritance. And now Jacob wants to make a profitable deal with his daughter's rapist. So yes, Shimon and Levi's actions may seem excessive, but they also come as somewhat of a relief that someone is finally sticking up for family.

The brothers' virtue lies not just in the act of revenge—which is gruesome and arguably disproportionate—but also in the anger that causes it. By adopting a prudent "what's done is done, and let's make the best of it" approach, Jacob shows nothing but a concern for his safety and profit. The two brothers, by contrast, are too outraged over the treatment of their sister to engage in a cost-benefit analysis. Their anger leads to a decidedly imprudent act of revenge, and it's the imprudence that demonstrates loyalty to their sister.

Now the second story. In the second presidential debate of 1988, CNN moderator Bernard Shaw put candidate Michael Dukakis on the spot. "Governor," Shaw asked, "if Kitty Dukakis were raped and murdered, would you favor an irrevocable death penalty for the killer?"

Dukakis replied, "No, I don't, Bernard, and I think you know that I've opposed the death penalty during all of my life. I don't see any evidence that it's a deterrent, and I think there are better and more effective ways to deal with violent crime. We've done so in my own state, and it's one of the reasons why we have had the biggest drop in crime of any industrial state in America, why we have the lowest murder rate of any industrial state in America."

At the time of the debate, Dukakis had been leading in the polls. Many pundits believe this answer was the single biggest cause of Dukakis's eventual defeat.

After the election, the conventional wisdom held that anyone who opposed the death penalty was unelectable. But opposition to the death penalty wasn't the real problem with Dukakis's response. Rather, it was the clinical nature of his answer to such a personal question. Like Jacob, Dukakis showed no depth of feeling, no anger, no fierce loyalty to a close family member. Kitty has been raped and killed, and Dukakis is worried about whether the death penalty is a deterrent? This is no time for a cost-benefit analysis. But now imagine if this had been Dukakis's response:

> Bernard, as you know, I've been against the death penalty all of my life. I don't think it's the state's business to end the lives of its citizens, no matter how heinous their actions. And I'll tell you something else: if Kitty had been raped and murdered, I wouldn't want the man executed by lethal injection fifteen years later, after dozens of appeals and legal challenges. I'd want to track down that son of a bitch before the law could get ahold of him and kill him myself with my bare hands. I'd think it was my job to do it, not some district attorney or judge or jury of twelve people who didn't even know her. Maybe society can't allow that to happen, but that's what I'd want to do in that situation.

This response would have allowed Dukakis to retain his opposition to the death penalty and turn the tables on those who accused him of being "soft on crime." Now it's the proponents of capital punishment who are clinical, cowardly, and "by the book." They're the ones who want a torturous legal bureaucracy to do what a decent husband should want to do himself. By tapping into virtuous qualities of revenge, Dukakis could have had the best of both worlds.

Critics of the death penalty often refer to it as "legalized revenge," but the truth is closer to the opposite. Honor cultures, as we've seen, think it's shameful when third parties punish people who have wronged them or their families. Revenge is personal. Most arguments against the death penalty involve deterrence and racial bias, and thus far arguments haven't resonated with a majority of the US population. Is the death penalty a deterrent? Probably not, but proponents can reply that it's not about deterrence; it's about justice. Is there racial bias in how the death penalty is applied? Absolutely. But advocates can reply that we must work to eliminate the racial bias, not prohibit the practice. But what if, like my hypothetical Dukakis, opponents called the death penalty dishonorable—a sign of cowardice and weakness? This challenge might have greater resonance, especially for people in the so-called honor states where capital punishment is most popular.

The point can broaden to the justice system as a whole. Like most issues in modern criminal punishment, the debate over the death penalty is premised on a fiction. When people say that "the death penalty is about justice," they're appealing to an illusion, a philosophically bankrupt ideal: the existence of "blind and impartial" justice. Honor cultures turn to revenge because they understand that justice isn't impartial but personal. How can we get the best of both worlds? How can we reorient our understanding of justice to reflect what's true and good about revenge without incurring its unacceptable costs? That is the subject of Chapter Six.

CHAPTER 6

HONORABLE JUSTICE

Justice, if it means anything, means getting people to feel it.

—WILLIAM IAN MILLER

Our current approach to criminal justice causes stupendous suffering for both victims and criminals. The illusory ideal of "blind and impartial" justice is an obstacle to effective reform. Honor-oriented justice rightly rejects this ideal. By understanding what honor gets right about justice and what we get wrong, we can remove these obstacles. The new movement called "restorative justice," which is modeled on honor-based approaches, holds great promise for improving our system of punishment. But adopting the movement requires that we abandon the core principles at the foundation of our current approach.

Clytemnestra's Ghost

In case you were wondering, Electra and Orestes get their revenge on Clytemnestra for murdering their father. For Sophocles (at least what exists of his corpus), the tragedy ends there. But in Aeschylus's version, Clytemnestra's death occurs in the second play of a trilogy known as the *Oresteia*. At the end of the second play, *The Libation Bearers*, Orestes is on the run after killing Clytemnestra, hunted by the ancient godlike vengeance spirits known as the Furies. The final play, *Eumenides*, begins with Orestes fleeing to the oracle of Delphi to ask the god Apollo for help.

    Eumenides is famous for presenting the first official criminal trial in Greek literature, the trial of Orestes for the crime of matricide. Most scholars interpret the play as heralding the triumph of law-governed, democratic, impartial, *real* justice over the honor and revenge-style justice in Homer's epics and the earlier tragedies. I'm skeptical of this interpretation. When you examine the proceedings of the trial, it looks a lot more like a travesty of justice than a triumph.

    Here's what happens. Athena sets up the trial with twelve randomly selected Athenians to serve as jurors. The Furies play the role of prosecutor, and Apollo represents the defendant, Orestes. Perhaps anticipating the modern criminal justice system, the trial devotes most of its attention to a technicality: whether Clytemnestra is *really* a parent of Orestes, whether Clytemnestra's blood really runs through his veins. Apollo, for the defense, argues that mother and son are not in fact blood relatives. Why? Because children share only their father's blood. The mother is a mere surrogate, a vessel for the father's blood. Orestes is therefore innocent of matricide. His evidence? Exhibit A: the goddess Athena herself sprang just from her father, Zeus—no mother required. "The man is the source of life," Apollo says, "the one who mounts" (antiquity's version of "If it doesn't fit, you must acquit").

Apollo's argument is plainly ludicrous. In all of existence, one woman doesn't have a mother, and she happens to be a goddess and the daughter of the most powerful god in the universe; therefore, no children share their mothers' blood. Yet that's the entirety of Orestes's defense. The trial offers no examination of Orestes's motives, mitigating factors, or culpability. Instead, it harps on irrelevant procedural details.

The jury's verdict reflects the arbitrariness of the proceedings: a perfectly even split, six for conviction, six for acquittal. With a hung jury, Athena breaks the tie—she votes for acquittal. Her reasoning? "I honor the male in all things except marriage. Yes, with all my heart I am my father's child." That is the so-called triumph of impartial justice. Athena is daddy's little girl, so she'll let Orestes off the hook for killing his mother.

Meanwhile, what's become of the victim during the proceedings? Clytemnestra is dead, of course, but her ghost had been present at the beginning of the play, telling the Furies to get off their butts and hunt down Orestes. Once the trial begins, Clytemnestra vanishes, never to be heard from again.

Clytemnestra's disappearance aptly reflects the place of victims in the modern criminal justice system. The two dominant Western theories of punishment—retributivism and utilitarianism—are polar opposites in virtually every way but one. They both share a total indifference to victims. Once an offense crosses the largely arbitrary line from civil to criminal trial, the conflict changes from one between a plaintiff and a defendant to one between the offender and "the people." The victim is removed from the equation.

Aeschylus had no illusions about why Athens turned to a state-run judicial system in place of family feuds. At the time that he's writing, the Greek world and Athens in particular are trying to form a cohesive community, a family of their own. They're trying to consolidate and build an empire. The intrafamily violence in the *Oresteia* is a metaphor for internal discord, civil war—something nations cannot afford during periods of international instability. "Here in our homeland," Athena tells the Furies, "never cast the stones that whet our bloodlust. Never pluck the heart of a battle cock and plant it in *our* people—intestine war seething against themselves. Let our wars wage on abroad, with all their force, to satisfy our powerful lust for fame." Take your fury, your bitterness, and your resentment onto the battlefield. Do that, Athena says, and you'll be honored. If Clytemnestra can't get justice, well, that's a small price to pay.

For Aeschylus, then, Orestes's trial isn't a triumph of impartial justice but a compromise between personal justice and internal harmony. He was honest about the reasons that trials should replace personal vengeance. We are not. We have concocted theories to convince ourselves that procedural justice, "blind and impartial" justice, is *true* justice. But the theories are full of empty principles on illusory foundations. And the unjust elements of Aeschylus's fictional trial have gotten much worse in the present day.

Our Broken Justice System

The American criminal justice system has produced a prison population of more than 2.3 million people. Prison conditions are atrocious and dehumanizing, which leads to high recidivism rates (close to 70 percent for property and drug crimes) that tear apart families and communities. Physical and sexual assault are pervasive. The racial imbalance is indefensible. The growth of private prisons gives corporations incentives to lobby for stricter enforcement and longer sentences to increase the prison population. Wealthy defendants obtain high-priced lawyers to exploit the bewildering array of procedures and statutes to benefit their clients, giving them an overwhelming advantage over poorer defendants. Oh, and take a guess what percentage of cases get resolved through plea bargains rather than trials. When you ask most people that question, they usually guess somewhere between 20 and 30 percent. The actual number is 97 percent. Fewer than three in one hundred cases go to trial. The other ninety-seven are the product of attorneys negotiating settlements. If even 10 percent of defendants took their cases to trial, the system would collapse from lack of personnel to adjudicate them.

This gruesome state of affairs causes stupendous suffering for both criminals and victims (not to mention taxpayers) and has few defenders from either side of the political spectrum. But what does all of this have to do with honor? Honor-oriented justice rightly rejects the illusory ideal that is at the foundation of our punishment system: the pursuit of "blind and impartial" justice. This ideal does not entail many of the abuses in our system, but, as we'll see, it presents formidable obstacles to effective reform. By understanding what honor gets right about justice, and what we get wrong, we can remove these obstacles.

The following shows three central ways in which honor approaches differ from the theories behind modern criminal justice:

Honor: Principles of justice are local and particular, grounded in the norms, feelings, and beliefs of the parties involved in the conflict and the surrounding community.

Modern criminal justice: Principles of justice are *universal*, objective, and derived through reason.

Honor: Conflicts are always between offenders and victims.

Modern criminal justice: When offenders commit crimes, the conflict is between the offender and the state, not the offender and the victim.

Honor: The aim of justice is to resolve a conflict between the offender and the victim, to make things right. Just verdicts must satisfy victims, restore honor to the relevant parties, and maintain harmony within the community.

Modern criminal justice: The aim of justice is to give offenders the punishment that is proportionate to their culpability. Offenders of equal culpability must receive equal punishment.

For the remainder of the chapter, I'll examine the philosophical defects in theories that ground our current system and then discuss an exciting new movement called restorative justice that incorporates the strengths and the truth of honorable justice.

"Uncharted Seas of Irrelevance": Culpability and the Role of the Victim

The central tenet of the modern justice system is a retributivist one: criminal offenders should receive their "just deserts"—the punishments that are proportionate to their culpability. Culpability has two components: the severity of the wrong and the offender's moral responsibility or blameworthiness. So, for example, imagine that Helen commits an act of armed robbery and assault. To determine Helen's culpability, you examine the severity of the crime (were her victims harmed, how much money did Helen steal, and what kind of weapon did she use?) and her moral responsibility (her mental state and other potentially mitigating factors). The feelings and desires of her victims are deemed irrelevant—because they don't factor into Helen's culpability. Indeed, knowledge about the victims can be regarded as *obstacles* to the pursuit of impartial justice, because such knowledge might lead juries to base their verdicts on emotion rather than reason, distorting their sense of the offender's culpability.

This perspective on victims held sway in the United States for much of its history. But in the middle of the twentieth century, a "victims' rights" movement emerged to combat the growing marginalization of victims in the criminal justice process. A Supreme Court ruling in 1973 laid the groundwork for the movement, holding that states could enact legislation that created a participatory role for victims. The Crimes Victims' Rights Act of 2004 granted rights to victims for the first time in US history.

The problem is that including victims in criminal justice process doesn't fit comfortably within the theoretical framework that grounds it. The ongoing controversy over victim-impact statements, or VIS, illustrates this tension. Victim-impact statements are statements that express the grief and suffering of crime victims and in some cases their desires concerning the offender's sentence. In the 1987 Supreme Court case *Booth v. Maryland*, the justices overturned a lower court's use of VIS for capital trials (cases that could lead to the death penalty). Justice Lewis Powell authored the majority decision. The Eighth Amendment, Powell writes, requires judges and juries to consider only evidence that has some bearing on the defendant's "personal responsibility and moral guilt." To do otherwise would create the risk that a death sentence would be based on considerations that are "constitutionally impermissible or totally irrelevant" to the sentencing process. "The focus of a VIS," Powell writes, "is not on the defendant, but on the character and reputation of the victim and the effect on his family. These factors may be *wholly unrelated to the blameworthiness of a particular defendant.*" The formal presentation of victim-impact evidence, he continues, "can serve no other purpose than to inflame the jury and divert it from deciding the case on the relevant evidence concerning the crime and the defendant," which is unacceptable, for "a sentence must be, and appear to be, based on reason, rather than caprice or emotion."

Powell argues that knowledge about the feelings of victims could lead to disproportionate punishments, which violates the Eighth

Amendment. Incidentally, nothing in the text of the Eighth Amendment mentions or even alludes to the issue of proportionality. The amendment prohibits cruel or unusual punishments and prohibits them whether they are proportionate or not. Nevertheless, there is plenty of judicial precedent for interpreting the Eighth Amendment as a demand for proportionality—in large part because it is a core feature of retributive theory.

Four years later, the Court reversed the ruling in *Payne v. Tennessee* and allowed the use of victim-impact statements. In a furious dissent, Justice Marshall wrote that the Court had abandoned "rules of relevance that are older than the Nation itself, and ventures into uncharted seas of *irrelevance*." The new decision, according to Marshall, allows the prosecutor to "introduce evidence that sheds no light on the defendant's guilt or moral culpability, and thus serves no purpose other than to encourage jurors to decide in favor of death rather than life on the basis of their emotions rather than their reason." Subsequent decisions, however, have tempered or reversed those rulings. The quest for victim participation in the criminal process has had more setbacks than gains.

Now, you might think that excluding victim-impact statements would help defendants in capital cases, by preventing victims from "inflaming" the juries and judges with vindictive anger. But more often, victims want the defendant's life to be spared. But these wishes are deemed irrelevant as well. In 1987 an Oklahoma family's testimony was excluded from consideration because it asked the jury not to impose the death penalty. In keeping with the *Booth* ruling, the judge ruled that the testimony was irrelevant because it related neither to the defendant's character nor to the circumstances of the offense (that is, the offender's culpability). "Such testimony," the ruling stated, "at best, would be a gossamer veil which would blur the jury's focus on the issue it must decide...because the offense was committed not against the victim but against the community as a whole." A Colorado judge in 2014 used this ruling to bar the parents of a murdered son from expressing their opposition to a death sentence for the son's killer to the jury.

The notion that the wishes of the people who suffered most from the crime would be irrelevant to the trial's outcome is one that exists only in cultures under the sway of retributive theory. In Iran, for example, a country not known for its merciful approach to criminals, the victims have until the moment of the execution to forgive the offender and commute the sentence to a prison term. The United States offers no such opportunity to victims, because doing so would contradict the principles of blind and impartial justice.

And here's the problem. The victims' rights movement was born out of advocacy, not philosophy. It was born out of frustration with being "nameless/faceless non-players in criminal justice system." The absence of theoretical support for victim participation has stalled the movement and paved the way for rulings that continue to ignore the victim's voice. So let's examine the three core principles that stand in the way of incorporating victims in criminal justice to see how well supported they truly are.

We've seen them in some form already. The first is the retributive demand that punishments be proportionate to the offender's culpability (as defined above) and that offenders of equal culpability should receive equal punishments. The second is what we might call the "dignity principle": that crimes are offenses not against victims but against the community, state, or the nation as a whole. The third principle is that verdicts should be based on reason rather than emotion. As we have seen, honor cultures reject all three of these principles. And for good reason. There are no good arguments for any of them.

Let's start with the first principle, the proportionality requirement. This principle has some well-known problems, most prominently: How on earth do we determine the quantum of punishment that is commensurate with a given crime? What is the deserved punishment for armed robbery? Ten years in prison? Fifteen years? Two years and probation? Flogging? Philosophers and legal theorists have struggled to find principled answers to these questions.

The most plausible option is to employ a "range-only" view of proportionality according to which a criminal's culpability determines only the upper and lower limits of deserved punishment, a view defended by criminologist Norval Morris. Morris points out that while we don't have a good sense of what precise quantum punishment is deserved, we do have a sense of when punishments can be undeserved (say, thirty years in prison for marijuana possession). According to Morris, particular crimes have a wide range of deserved punishments, and we should use utilitarian considerations to determine punishments within that range.

Morris's account is flawed, but at least it lacks the pretense to precision shared by many of its competitors. According to prominent desert theorist Andrew Von Hirsch, however, Morris's view is open to "a fundamental objection": it would allow two offenders who are equally culpable to receive different punishments (thus violating the retributive principle). But Von Hirsch agrees with Morris that it's impossible to match units of deserved punishments to particular crimes. So he faces a dilemma. His proposed solution employs a distinction between cardinal and ordinal proportionality. Cardinal proportionality is "range only," issuing upper and lower limits beyond which punishments would obviously be either too severe or too light. Ordinal proportionality demands consistency in punishment. It's meant to ensure that criminals who are equally culpable receive the same punishment.

Von Hirsch calls the demand for consistency a "basic requirement of fairness," and it may seem plausible when considered abstractly or in the form of hypothetical scenarios. But the plausibility diminishes when it's applied to cases in the real world. Consider a recent trial in Grand Junction, Colorado. A woman was driving in the early morning, drunk and high on meth. On the way, she had an accident and hit a sanitation worker. The victim's legs were shattered, and he subsequently endured ten surgeries to repair them. The worker testified during the woman's trial and asked the judge to give the woman a lenient sentence. He told the judge he could relate to her predicament, that he had been in a dark place once too, and hoped she could eventually get to a better place, just as he had. The prosecutors and the judge took his wishes into account and dismissed the most serious charges. The woman received the minimum sentence allowable—still more than five years in jail.

Here we have a clear violation of the principle of consistency. Many people in Colorado have been given much higher sentences for equally culpable behavior. But did the judge and prosecutor violate a "basic requirement of fairness"? Is this case clearly unjust? The victim—the only one who was harmed by the offense—is more satisfied than he would be with a higher sentence. He feels respected by the process, and the woman still receives a punishment within a reasonable cardinal range. If anything, this verdict seems considerably *more* just than a verdict that ignored the victim's wishes would be.

So maybe our commitment to consistency isn't so deep after all. Indeed, outside of the context of criminal justice, we seem to lack it entirely. If two husbands in relatively happy marriages betray their wives on a business trip, no one finds it remotely unjust if their wives respond differently—if one decides to give the husband another chance and the other boots him out and demands a separation. And no one would dream of claiming that the wife's wishes were irrelevant. Everyday life is filled with cases like this—acts of infidelity, betrayals of trust, insulting or offensive remarks, and so forth. We don't expect equally culpable offenders to receive the same amount of blame or punishment. We expect people to stay within certain boundaries in their responses, but within those boundaries we leave it up to the relevant parties to determine the appropriate responses. Yet once we're in the realm of criminal justice, the demand for consistency allegedly becomes a core principle of fairness.

Why such different demands and expectations for the two kinds of conflicts? It's not fully clear, but one part of the answer is laudable. A core principle of most Western democracies is equal treatment from the state. Since the state issues the punishment, it seems unjust for two offenders of equal culpability to receive different punishments. In this sense, consistency matters. But it isn't an overriding consideration. It's one consideration among many, and arguably a minor one at that. Fairness requires the state to take both offenders *and* victims into account. Victims, after all, are the ones who actually suffer from the crime. And they are affected by crimes in different ways. Victims have different needs, desires, feelings about what happened. Victim interests are also relevant to justice and fairness. But our system doesn't recognize this.

These points seem obvious and intuitive, and they've been made over and over again by the victims' movement. The common reply appeals to the second core principle, what I called the "dignity principle": crimes are not offenses against victims but rather offenses against "the people" or "the state." On one level, the principle is clearly false. If a man assaults me with a broken bottle and slices my face, the state doesn't end up with a scarred face—I do. Nobody denies this. The claim that crimes are offenses against the state rather than a victim is meant as a metaphor. But it's not at all clear what the metaphor is supposed to represent or why it should result in the decidedly nonmetaphorical exclusion of victims' interests.

Another reply appeals to the third principle: that verdicts should be based on reason rather than emotion. The desires of victims are often based on emotions; punishment should be based on reason. Recall Justice Powell's claim that victim-impact evidence could inflame the jury and must be excluded because "a sentence must be, and appear to be, based on reason, rather than caprice or emotion." Or Sandra Day O'Connor, who in a decision concerning mitigating evidence in capital cases, writes, "The sentence imposed at the penalty stage should reflect a reasoned moral response to the defendant's background, character, and crime rather *than mere sympathy or emotion.*" Determining the appropriateness of the death penalty, according to O'Connor, "is a moral inquiry into the culpability of the defendant, and not an emotional response to the mitigating evidence."

Statements like this are grounded in the idea that only reason can determine culpability. Emotions are distorting, "at best...a gossamer veil which would blur the jury's focus." This might seem plausible if it weren't for one inconvenient detail: no one has ever provided a remotely compelling rationalist (reason-based) argument for establishing an offender's culpability. Here, for example, is Hegel—perhaps the foremost retributivist in the rationalist tradition—explaining why wrongdoers deserve to be punished.

> Right as something absolute cannot be set aside, and so committing a crime is in principle a nullity: and this nullity is the essence of what a crime effects. A nullity, however, must reveal itself to be such, i.e. manifest itself as vulnerable. A crime, as an act, is not something positive, not a first thing, on which punishment would supervene as a negation. It is something negative, so that its punishment is only a negation of the negation. Right in its actuality, then, annuls what infringes it and therein displays its validity and proves itself to be a necessary, mediated, reality.

It's tough to have a clue what Hegel is talking about, never mind buy into the program. Try to apply Hegel's idea to the context of a real crime—say, the shooting of Laura Blumenfeld's father from Chapter Five. The crime, according to Hegel, is a nullity, a vulnerable nullity, and the punishment (Omar's prison term) was a negation of that nullity, through which Right proves itself to be a necessary, mediated reality. Hegel's influence would be comical if it hadn't played such a big role in producing our retributive system of justice.

The more recent, more comprehensible, versions of rationalist punishment theories fare no better. Herbert Morris's "fair-play" account, for example, is credited with sparking the retributivist revival in criminal justice in the late 1960s and early '70s. According to Morris, fairness requires a roughly equal distribution of benefits and burdens in a society. One of these burdens is having to restrain ourselves from interfering with other people enjoying their benefits. By not taking on the burden of restraint, criminals help themselves to an unfair share of the benefits of society. Punishment, Morris claims, removes their unfair advantage.

This theory is riddled with problems. For one, it assumes that individuals in our society start out with roughly equal distribution of benefits and burdens. One visit to a failing inner-city school would cure anyone of this view. But even if you granted the assumption, Morris's view fails to establish the principles of consistency or proportionality. For most of us, refraining from murder or sexual assault is not a "burden," since we don't have a desire to perform these actions in the first place. Does that mean that less tempting, more brutal crimes require less punishment? And that more tempting crimes like fraud or tax evasion require more?

A third rationalist alternative derives from Immanuel Kant and later John Rawls. This theory asks us to imagine that we are in a hypothetical position under a "veil of ignorance" that conceals all of the particular facts about our lives: we don't know whether we'll be poor or rich, smart or dumb, greedy or moderate, criminals or law-abiding citizens. The truly just system of punishment, according to this view, is the one that rational people would choose in this hypothetical position. And take a wild guess which system we would choose, according to the theory's proponents. That's right: rational agents would opt for a retributivist system that punishes people precisely according to their culpability. (So that worked out nicely.)

Most objections to this approach argue that with such little knowledge of who we are under a veil of ignorance, we lack the basis to make a choice about punishment institutions. But setting this objection aside, why think that our rational, stripped-down selves would indeed choose retributivism over available alternatives that involve the victim? Rational agents in the original position are just as likely to be victims as criminals—why would they opt for a system that ignores their interests entirely?

The obvious flaws in these approaches point to a fundamental dishonesty in the rationalist project. They begin with a strong emotional conviction that offenders ought to be punished according to the three retributive principles. And they develop elaborate post hoc theories designed to reach their conclusions. But the theories have obvious flaws. Like it or not, reason is insufficient for establishing how the state should address criminal wrongdoing. Emotions must be a part of any theory of punishment too. The only question is whether we're honest enough to acknowledge this. Honor cultures have no illusions about the emotional component of justice and thus have a lot to teach us about how to incorporate them.

Honorable Punishment: Restorative Justice

There's a popular Reddit website called "Justice Porn" where members post videos of people getting their just deserts. The site describes itself as a "place to see bullies getting their comeuppance," and the most popular videos feature bullies getting beaten up by their intended victims. These videos have several features that make them satisfying. First, the bully suffers the same treatment that he (or very occasionally she) was intending to inflict. So the suffering is proportionate to the harm they intended to cause and have almost certainly caused in the past. Second, the bullies learn how it feels to be one of their victims and maybe get morally educated as a result. Third, the victims stand up to their tormenters. We watch them gain self-respect and the respect of onlookers and in some cases even the bully in the process. Any one of these features can arouse our sense of justice, but when you put them all together, you get justice porn.

Our criminal justice system captures the first two of the features but not the third. Crime victims often suffer a feeling of powerlessness and a loss of respect. When victims fight back, we applaud their courage and honor. Defenders of the status quo often assume that punishing wrongdoers automatically restores the self-respect of victims by sending a message to the offender that the victim is a person whose rights cannot be violated. But this is a rationalist fantasy with no basis in real human psychology. Psychologist Dale Miller has shown that the way victims respond to insults and offenses affects their self-image and their image in the eyes of others. We've seen how many honor cultures actively shun third-party punishment for precisely this reason. There aren't any justice-porn videos of victims reporting the bully to the school principal and the bully getting suspended.

Of course, the ethics of the schoolyard offers only so much insight into the nature of justice. We cede the role of punisher to the state in large part to prevent victim retaliation and vigilantism. But we don't do this for reasons involving justice. We do it for practical reasons—to prevent escalating feuds and to limit collateral damage. But crime victims suffer costs when their cases are handled entirely by the state, and a maximally just approach to criminal punishment would consider the interests of crime victims while at the same time retaining societal order and the rule of law. By rejecting any special voice for victims, our current system fails to do this. So let's examine an alternative model—restorative justice—that directly involves the victim in the sentencing process.

Restorative justice is a recent movement that takes direct aim at the depersonalized, excessively rationalistic nature of the current legal system. Restorative processes vary across domains and cultures, but they all share the following essential principles. First, crimes should be viewed as conflicts between individuals and only secondarily as violations against the state. Second, the aim of criminal justice is to repair the harms, resolve the conflicts, and restore harmony within the community. The aim of the legal system as a whole is to enable the stakeholders in the conflict—the victim, offender, families, and other community members—to actively participate in the attempt to find a resolution. The fundamental difference between conventional and restorative justice, writes legal ethicist Charles Barton, involves empowerment of the key stakeholders, "so that the matter is resolved in ways that are meaningful and right for them."

Models for implementation vary across domains as well, but most of them contain some sort of victim-offender mediation conference, sometimes referred to as "restorative circles," in which victims, offenders, and other stakeholders address the harm and try to resolve the conflict. Each person in the conference has a chance to speak. Victims can ask questions of the offender and relate the ways in which they were harmed. Offenders are encouraged to take responsibility for the harm. They aren't compelled to apologize, or to express remorse, or to answer the victim's questions—but they're given the opportunity to do so if they wish. Family, friends, and other members of the affected community are given the opportunity to speak as well. After speaking, the participants try to come up with ways to repair the harm through restitution, community service, and prison time if necessary. Trained facilitators or mediators preside over the conference and are required to take all of the participants' interests into account. Most restorative programs also devote resources to reintegrating the offender into the community once they have paid their debts and obligations.

It's no coincidence that restorative approaches bear striking similarities to the approaches of honor cultures. (Look back at the list on page 158 and you'll see that the core principles are virtually identical.) The methods of tribal communities for conflict resolution serve as the model for restorative justice. Although honor cultures are more famous for their bloody feuds, the fact is that feuds are costly and people want to avoid them as long as they can maintain their honor and self-respect. With such high stakes, honor groups acquire tremendous skills and techniques for mediation, for discovering nonviolent ways for all parties to save face and restore their honor. Revenge is one form of restorative justice but not the preferred one, by any means.

Restorative justice isn't designed to be a panacea or a total replacement of the current legal system. Restorative approaches may not be appropriate for certain crimes, because of unwilling participants, the absence of identifiable victims, or other reasons. Most jurisdictions have a separate impartial criminal process for determining guilt that precedes the restorative phase of the sentencing. During this process, the judge may set boundaries for the outcome of the restorative phase and upper and lower limits on a prison sentence. This ensures that offenders' rights are respected and that the outcomes are consistent with the norms and values of society as well as the law.

Critics have several categories of objections to restorative justice. Some object that it's too soft and touchy-feely, too easy on the offenders—"justice for pussies," as one prominent legal theorist told me. They consider it naive and disrespectful to expect victims and offenders to "hug it out" after a crime. This objection completely misunderstands the nature and purpose of restorative justice—and only people who have never seen it in action could offer it with a straight face. What's tougher on offenders? Sitting in a courtroom while lawyers and behavioral science experts—complete strangers—battle over the legal minutia of your crime? Or having to face your victims and their families and look them in the eye? Not surprisingly, many offenders initially resist the idea of personal contact with their victims, because they're reluctant to reckon with the human cost of their actions. The current system lets them off the hook.

Another common objection to restorative justice is that it's *too hard* on offenders, that it humiliates them and fails to respect their dignity as human beings. Restorative justice is hard on the offenders, but that's only part of the story. Restorative conferences allow offenders to explain the reasons behind their actions, to express genuine remorse, and to offer forms of restitution. Restorative justice, writes one of its godfathers, Nils Christie, gives the offender an opportunity "to change his position from being a listener to a discussion—often a highly unintelligible one—of how much pain he ought to receive, into a participant in a discussion of how he could make it good again." Restorative justice treats offenders as people rather than cases, as members of the moral community.

Some critics worry that the encounters will be too difficult for victims, resulting in "secondary victimization." This is a legitimate concern, but one that's addressed by making the process voluntary. In most models, both victims and offenders must give their consent to a conference; otherwise, the sentence is determined through more

traditional means. (Offenders may be offered incentives to participate, but the incentives shouldn't make it too tempting for them
to offer phony expressions of remorse.) In addition, studies show
that most victims welcome the opportunity to participate in their
own conflicts. The results of a recent Canadian survey indicate that
89 percent of violent crime victims wanted to meet the offenders.
Even in what seems like the most problematic type of crime—sexual
assault—victims report positive effects from meeting with offenders.
Victims who participated in restorative conferences showed a decrease in PTSD symptoms. Survivors reported that the "experience
was empowering rather than traumatizing." In another recent study,
70 percent of rape survivors reported that they would welcome the
opportunity for victims to be able to meet with their offenders in
conference settings.

Honor cultures understand the empowering effects of these encounters for victims very well. We learn a lot about ourselves from
how we handle ourselves in conflicts. Meeting with offenders allows
victims to express courage and pride and self-respect. As Christie
puts it, the current legal system "steals the conflict" from victims by
regarding crimes as offenses against the state:

> The victim is a particularly heavy loser in this situation. Not
> only has he suffered, lost materially or become hurt, physically
> or otherwise. And not only does the state take the compensation.
> But above all he has lost participation in his own Case. It is the
> Crown that appears in the newspaper, very seldom the victim.
> It is the Crown that gets a chance to talk to the offender, and

neither the Crown nor the offender are particularly interested in carrying on that conversation. The prosecutor is fed-up long since. The victim would not have been. *He might have been scared to death, panic-stricken, or furious. But he would not have been uninvolved. It would have been one of the important days in his life.*

Active participation in conflicts can be scary, panic inducing, infuriating, and emotionally charged. Victims may have to overcome fear or blind fury to face their victimizers and look them in the eye. We learn what we're made of in these situations. These encounters help victims recover their self-respect—not just in theory but in practice.

The interactions also provide opportunities for victims and offenders to express empathy, to recognize the humanity in one another. Offenders get a more genuine sense of the suffering they've caused. And victims come to better understand the reasons behind the offender's actions, which may lead to partial forgiveness. Or they may still hate the person who wronged them. And the offenders may feel the same contempt for their victims. Either way, they're compelled to deal with real human beings in a way that is well beyond anything our current legal system has to offer. The same holds for family and other community members who attend the meetings. Restorative justice offers a chance for active engagement with people with different backgrounds and experiences.

Another worry about restorative justice is the potential for racial bias to influence restorative outcomes. Again, this is a legitimate worry, but we must evaluate it in light of existing evidence rather than speculation. And we must examine whether restorative justice is more vulnerable to the effects of racial bias than the status quo. I've already discussed the endemic racial bias in the criminal justice system. In the schools, "equitable" policies like zero tolerance for misbehavior have led to a massive disproportional number of suspensions for minority and especially African American students. The suspensions are the primary engine of the school-to-prison pipeline, which again disproportionately affects poor African American students. And the draconian school discipline policies can blur the lines between schools and prisons by turning "public schools into well-policed fortresses" and resulting in increasingly large numbers of school-based arrests. At this stage, the worries about racial bias are purely speculative. Restorative justice is a recent movement, and more empirical work needs to be done to gauge the effects of racial bias on restorative processes. But given the systematic and structural biases that infect our current disciplinary practices, it would be difficult for restorative justice to fare any worse.

The most common objection to restorative justice has been discussed briefly above: it violates the principle of consistency (or ordinal proportionality, in Von Hirsch's terminology). Restorative justice, almost by definition, must reject the principle that offenders of equal culpability should receive the same punishment. Each set of victims and offenders has different needs, wishes, temperaments, and personalities, and restorative outcomes will vary accordingly. Philosopher Michael Moore, a leading retributivist, argues that this disqualifies victim involvement. As he puts it, "In a truly victim-oriented system, if a wrongdoer has the good luck to injure one of those new testament types, instead of one of the old testament types, then that wrongdoer is going to receive less punishment—because he is always going to get the turn-your-other-cheek forgiveness response from his victim." Moore's point is that it's obviously unfair for the wrongdoer with the "new-testament type" victim to receive a reduced sentence, while the latter gets a higher one. But the intuitive appeal of this example derives from its hypothetical nature and the depiction of victims as caricatured "types" rather than complex people.

To really test our intuitions about consistency, we must evaluate them in light of real cases. Braithwaite, for example, in "In Search of Restorative Jurisprudence," describes a case of assault and attempted robbery in New Zealand in which the offender, Mr. Clotworthy, inflicted six stab wounds and a collapsed lung on the victim. The victim and offender agreed to have a restorative justice conference as an alternative to a traditional trial to see if the two could work out a satisfactory resolution. During the conference, the two parties and the presiding judge agreed upon the following sentence: Mr. Clotworthy would pay a compensation order of fifteen thousand dollars to pay for cosmetic surgery for the victim. He would also perform two hundred hours of community work and serve a two-year prison term that might be suspended if Clotworthy performed the work and paid the compensation. The sentence then went to the court of appeals. The appeals judges questioned the victim about the leniency of the sentence. The victim "reiterated his previous stance, emphasizing his wish to obtain funds for the necessary cosmetic surgery and his view that imprisonment would achieve nothing either for himself or Mr. Clotworthy." The judges were not convinced. They quashed the compensation order as well as the community service and instead sentenced Mr. Clotworthy to four years in prison. The victim "got neither his act of grace nor the money for his surgery."

The verdict in the court of appeals adheres more closely to the principle of consistency. Clotworthy got a more similar sentence to other offenders who had committed a similar crime. But is it a more just verdict? Not to me anyway. The appeals verdict seems considerably less just than the original verdict that respected the victim's wishes and repaired the harm to a significant degree.

Even in the most problematic example of homicide, our justice intuitions often side with the restorative model. Consider the case of Conor McBride, described in a recent *New York Times Magazine* article by Paul Tullis:

> At 2:15 in the afternoon on March 28, 2010, Conor McBride, a tall, sandy-haired 19-year-old wearing jeans, a T-shirt and New Balance sneakers, walked into the Tallahassee Police Department and approached the desk in the main lobby. Gina Maddox, the officer on duty, noticed that he looked upset and asked him how she could help. "You need to arrest me," McBride answered. "I just shot my fiancée in the head." When Maddox, taken aback, didn't respond right away, McBride added, "This is not a joke."

It wasn't a joke. About an hour earlier, at his parents' house, McBride had shot Ann Margaret Grosmaire, his girlfriend of three years. They were both students at Tallahassee Community College. The couple had been fighting for thirty-eight straight hours—in person, by text message, and over the phone. They fought about the mundane things that many couples might fight about. Instead of resolving their differences or shaking them off, they kept it up for two nights and two mornings, and it culminated in the moment that McBride shot Grosmaire.

Ann Grosmaire died in the hospital four days later. In Florida, the crime of first-degree murder typically carries a life sentence or the death penalty. However, the prosecutor can also charge the offender with a lesser crime such as manslaughter, which carries a much lighter sentence. In the weeks following the crime, Ann's parents and Conor's parents had become close. (They had met in the hospital by Ann's bedside.) As the trial drew near, the Grosmaires learned about the restorative justice movement and asked the prosecutor, Jack Campbell, if they could do a restorative conference with Conor McBride and his parents. They asked Campbell to base his decision on the plea offer on the outcome of the conference. Restorative justice was a relatively foreign notion in Florida and had never even been considered for a serious crime. But since the request came from the victim's parents, Campbell agreed.

During the conference everyone had an opportunity to speak without interruptions. The Grosmaires spoke first. They described their love for Ann and the tremendous suffering they had experienced since the crime. According to Sujatha Baliga, the mediator of the conference, Ann's mother "did not spare [Conor] in any way the cost of what he did. There were no kid gloves, none. It was really, really tough. Way tougher than anything a judge could say." Then it was Conor's turn to speak. He described the crime and surrounding circumstances in harrowing detail. He did not shirk responsibility in any way. On the contrary, his account was even worse than the Grosmaires imagined. He disclosed that Ann had been on her knees and pleading with him not to shoot when he pulled the trigger. Tullis writes: "As Conor told the story, Andy's [Anne's father] whole body began to shake. 'Let me get this right,' he said, and asked Conor about Ann being on her knees.... Conor answered, clarifying precisely how helpless Ann was at the moment he took her life."

After each member had spoken, each person had the opportunity to suggest a punishment. Before the conference the Grosmaires had indicated that they would ask for a light sentence of five years in prison. But after hearing Conor's story, they asked for more prison time. Kate Grosmaire suggested five to fifteen years. Andy Grosmaire suggested ten to fifteen years. Conor's parents agreed with Andy about the higher sentence. Conor did not suggest a sentence because "he did not think he should have a say."

In most restorative justice proceedings, the judge will issue a decision that reflects the consensus of the relevant parties. But since this was the first restorative justice case in Florida for such a serious crime, Jack Campbell promised only that he would take the opinions into account for determining the plea offer. Campbell honored his promise, offering a plea of twenty years in prison with five years' probation.

Like the original verdict in the Clotworthy trial, the outcome of this case is incompatible with the principle of consistency. The sentence was considerably lighter than the norm for homicides in Florida. Again, however, it seems more appropriate and more *just*

for Campbell to take the restorative conference into account in determining the plea offer. The possibility that an equally culpable homicide offender could receive a more severe sentence (because of the
wishes of a more vindictive family) doesn't undermine this intuition
in the least.

I'm not claiming that consistency should play *no* role in the
eventual outcome. If the Grosmaires had asked for a suspended sentence, or even a two- to five-year sentence, the judge might justly
reject this as too lenient in light of the sentences for other homicides of this kind. Restorative approaches entail only that consistent
sentencing is not an *overriding* consideration. It is just one consideration among many.

Let me conclude with a brief illustration from the great western
novel *Shane*. In the story, a cattle rancher named Fletcher is trying to strong-arm the resident homesteaders to sell their fertile land
to him. When the homesteaders refuse, Fletcher hires a notorious
gunman named Wilson to intimidate them. Joe Starrett, the inspirational leader of the homesteaders, has been able to keep the others from selling. But their courage is waning. Meanwhile, Shane, a
former gunman himself, has been staying at the Starrett household
as their guest. In the final pages of the novel, the situation comes to
a head, and Joe decides to face Wilson in a gunfight. Shane, however, realizes that Joe is outmatched and offers to face him himself. Joe thanks him but refuses. "It's my stand," Joe says. "Fletcher
is making a play against me. It's my business." Shane replies that
gunfighting is his kind of business and not Joe's. Joe replies, "And

where will it leave me? I couldn't hold my head up around here anymore. They'd say I ducked and they'd be right."

Joe's point is that if Shane fights this battle for him, people will rightly think he is a coward. For Joe, having the reputation of a coward is much worse than risking his life. He may die in the gunfight with Wilson, but he'll die with courage and honor. Shane recognizes the dilemma, but he has a solution. He provokes Joe into a fight and cold-cocks him with a gun. Shane then ties an unconscious Joe up and goes off to kill Wilson himself. Why does Shane tie Joe up? Because it is the only way for Joe to keep his self-respect in spite of the fact that Shane has fought the final battle. Now the homesteaders will know that Joe was *unable* to fight the battle himself. Shane recognizes this is not the ideal outcome, but he believes the alternative—Joe's certain death—is even worse.

For some crimes, the state can and should play the role of Shane, stealing the conflict and taking the punishment entirely out of the hands of the victim. For the majority of crimes, however, the state can play the more valuable role of mediator, offering victims the opportunity to display real courage and fortitude in resolving their own conflicts with their offenders.

Restorative justice offers a perfect illustration of how honor-related values, when properly contained, can bring tremendous benefits to modern society. In the final chapter, we'll look at other ways of containing honor and harnessing its virtues.

CHAPTER 7

HONOR CONTAINED

Honor, at its best, promotes individual virtues like courage, self-reliance, hospitality, and personal integrity. Honor contributes to a sense of community, solidarity, and collective responsibility. When properly harnessed and directed, honor can advance social progress; it can unify oppressed groups and provide effective frameworks for resistance and reform. Well-functioning honor cultures exhibit great wisdom in handling conflicts in a wide range of contexts: from rural neighborhood bars to inner-city schools and even the criminal justice system. Honor can provide a sense of purpose in an increasingly atomized, alienating, and materialistic society. Honor, at its best, can help us lead better, richer, more meaningful lives.

The problem, though, lies in all those caveats—"at its best," "well functioning," and so forth. The same features that encourage community, loyalty, and sacrifice can also promote hatred, hostility, and prejudice. They can provoke and sustain long cycles of revenge. Honor codes may impose heavy burdens, a need to project images of toughness or purity that may not suit our personalities and attributes. Honor can restrict our autonomy, telling us what roles to adopt, whom to marry, what friends are acceptable, which enemies to hate. If we want to incorporate honor values into modern life, we must contain those values in ways that limit their moral costs while making the most of their moral advantages.

Honor's Hazards

Broadly speaking, the moral hazards of honor fall into two categories. The first is what I'll call the danger of escalation. The heightened sensitivity to insult in honor cultures, along with norms for violent retaliation in response to perceived disrespect, can lead to explosive situations and interactions. Think Tommy in *Goodfellas*, the character played by Joe Pesci (based on the real-life Mafia figure Tommy DeSimone). You're having some laughs, playing poker or out for a few drinks at a bar, and then one "Go get your fuckin' shinebox" or "Why don't you go fuck yourself" later, you're digging graves. This hazard increases exponentially at the group level. The same admirable virtues that honor tends to promote—such as courage, loyalty, solidarity, the willingness to risk injury or death to defend your group—can lead to escalating feuds between individuals, families, and entire communities. With no impartial, centralized authorities to impose constraints, the brutality and violence may intensify into a never-ending quest to get even.

The second category of moral hazards is an even deeper concern. All honor groups have norms for determining how honor is allocated and norms that encourage and prohibit certain kinds of behavior. But honor, unlike dignity, places few restrictions on the moral content of these norms. At the worst end of the spectrum, honor norms can sanction white nationalism, ethnic cleansing, or honor killings, the murders of women suspected of having extramarital sex by family members. When the content of honor norms is bad, their tremendous motivational power becomes an evil rather than a good, leading people to commit cruel and unjust actions out of a perverse sense of duty.

These dangers are serious and real. If they can't be contained, then honor's critics may prove to be right. But the hazards can be contained, and this chapter examines some models for doing so. Successful containment models address the hazards on two levels. First, they restrict the content of honor norms to rule out plainly immoral behavior and preserve respect for human rights. And second, they impose limits on aggression to keep it from escalating out of control. They accomplish both goals while at the same time preserving the flexibility of honor codes with minimal outside interference.

You might have noticed a tension in that last sentence. On the one hand, the models must constrain and limit the content of honor norms—which requires an external, largely impartial authority. On the other hand, they seek to minimize the role of external authorities to preserve the features that allow honor to work its magic. Striking the right balance between these aims is tricky business, but it's not impossible. We've seen one example already in the previous chapter, restorative justice. Now let's turn to some other examples of well-contained honor frameworks and see what lessons we can draw from them.

Civilized Insanity

Oddly enough, one of the best examples of a containment model in action is professional hockey. As we saw in Chapter One, hockey has a well-established honor code. Ross Bernstein, author of the definitive book on the code, describes it as a sacred covenant with "unwritten rules of engagement that had been handed down from generation to generation...[a] mysterious chain of accountability that [deals] with the issues of violence and fighting." Versions of the code exist at every level of play, from the professional to the amateur to the children's leagues. The code is embraced by players, coaches, and officials. "It's a living, breathing thing among us," says former enforcer Marty McSorley. "It changed and evolved as the rules changed and evolved, and it took on a life of its own."

The most famous (or infamous) aspect of the code is the sanctioning of in-game fights. The NHL is the only professional sports league that allows fighting to occur "within reason." Commentators often characterize this part of the code as a cynical ploy to appeal to the bloodlust of fans. In reality, though, fighting effectively makes an inherently violent game *less* violent and more just. "Spontaneous fights," writes Bernstein, "are considered to be a relatively safe release of emotions for players who might otherwise settle their differences with dangerous stick work." Allowing players to release pent-up emotions on the spot, in front of officials, is safer than letting those aggressions fester.

"Hockey is a game that polices itself," says McSorley, "and there is a lot of honor behind that." And, indeed, hockey has all the elements of a well-functioning honor culture. Its norms are fluid and flexible. They celebrate and reward paradigmatic honor values like courage, honesty, self-respect, respect for opponents, handling your business, and measured retaliation. The code insists on personal accountability. "The basic premise of the code," writes McSorley, "is that you have to answer for your actions on the ice." To this end, hockey has norms of collective responsibility, which encourages self-policing within the team. When a midlevel player or agitator takes a cheap shot on the opponent's superstar, the agitator knows—and his teammates know—that he's drawn a bulls-eye on their own superstar. But in common with most honor cultures, the self-policing goes on in private, in the locker room after the game. During the game, the code expects players to stand up and fight for their teammates even when they're in the wrong. Enforcer Tony Twist writes that he would fight for his teammates during games regardless of who he was or what he'd done: "It didn't matter if I didn't like a certain guy on my team or if I didn't agree with what I was fighting over. If we were wearing the same color sweater, then I was going to defend him no matter what." Attitudes like these cement bonds among teammates and between players and fans.

The fluidity of hockey's honor code makes it a constant source of debate and drama. In 1992, for example, the league office wanted to curb excessive fighting. So they instituted the "instigator rule," which gives an extra two-minute penalty to players who initiate fights. The rule reshaped the fighting landscape in the NHL, and everyone had an opinion on it. Before the rule, teams would designate a roster spot for "goons"—players whose only job was to intimidate opposing players and keep them from taking cheap shots at their teammates. It didn't matter if they barely knew how to skate; their presence and violent reputations would often be enough to keep the game clean. But then the occasional fights began to escalate when teams disagreed over whether the code had been violated. The goons were compelled to settle scores, and a single game could feature multiple team-wide brawls. The brawls were popular with the players, and the fans loved them, but the league believed that goons made the game too violent and low scoring. Some fights would spin out of control, spilling outside the rink (the great Bruins-Canadiens "Brawl in the Hall," for example), generating bad media attention and threats of legal interference. The instigator rule was designed to prevent this. Once the rule was in place, goons lost their value and were replaced by enforcers, who could contribute in other ways on the ice.

Many players and coaches hate the instigator rule. They think it frees up agitators to agitate with no accountability. Agitators enjoy taking liberties with opposing skill players, insulting them to get in their heads "and then running and hiding after dishing out dangerous hits." Barry Melrose, one of the rule's most ardent opponents, writes:

> Nowadays, players don't have to be accountable for their actions and they don't have to fight. Players can high-stick each other, spear each other, slash each other in the face, run each other from behind into the boards, and do so with the understanding that they can get away with it.... Twenty years ago if you ever sticked a guy and then not fought, your own teammates would

ostracize you and just wouldn't accept you in the locker room. A guy who turtled after doing something dirty would just not be accepted by his teammates. They would be embarrassed to have him on their team. And let me be clear, it didn't matter if you won or lost your fight, but you had to be accountable. You had to show up. If you did something dirty then you stood up like a man and you defended your actions; players at least respect that. Now players don't even have to show up and that in my eyes is a very sad thing. It is sad because it is just accepted.

Melrose's remarks reflect the recurring theme in honor cultures discussed in Chapter Four: it doesn't matter much whether you win a fight; what matters is that you show up and take responsibility.

Like most efforts to contain honor-fueled behavior, the instigator rule is controversial. Honor communities tend to resent outside forces meddling with their own way of dishing out justice. But since the NHL is a well-functioning honor culture, it has outlets for players and coaches to express their opinions on the rule and help the league revise and improve it. As it evolves, the players adapt, adding more drama and interest to a fascinating sport.

Most important for containing the danger of escalation in the NHL are the game officials. The referees and linesmen provide space for players to sort out conflicts, while keeping the violence "within reason." Officials have to understand and respect the code and to know when they should interfere to prevent the violence from going too far. It's just part of the job for these guys, Bernstein writes, "and they relish the close bonds that they foster with the various enforcers they work with on a daily basis." The bonds they form with the players allow officials to discern the crucial particulars of each conflict—when players are hurt or tired or so angry as to be dangerous. They have to be amateur psychologists, massaging egos, "constantly reassuring each player that he won and definitely came out on top." Otherwise, the players will have their rematches lined up before they get to the penalty box, which could lead to "a risk of having those situations escalate, involving more players and more chaos."

Hockey's approach to player aggression stands in sharp contrast to that of the National Basketball Association. After the NBA's most notorious out-of-control fight in 2004—the so-called "Malice in the Palace" between the Indiana Pacers and the Detroit Pistons, an on-court brawl that had fans throwing things at the players and players going after fans in the stands—the NBA imposed strict rules against fighting, a zero-tolerance policy. Today, any player who leaves the bench during a scuffle is automatically fined and suspended for the next game, no exceptions. Hockey officials, by contrast, are instructed to use discretion and judgment. Officials are there "to keep the peace and to prevent the games from getting out of hand," Bernstein writes, "but they know that the game polices itself, and they know that the code is there for a reason, so they play their role accordingly." Hockey officials play the role of mediator rather than judge, and consequently the players consider them part of their own community. The best hockey officials are exemplars for sustaining and containing an honor culture. We can learn a lot from the way they handle conflict in other domains of society.

Informal Social Control: Gang Violence

Hockey is a well-functioning honor culture, but it has many built-in advantages contributing to its success. For one thing, hockey's norms aren't too far out of line with the norms of the broader North American society. Hockey teams also have a good mix of younger players and respected veterans to keep them in line. And like all sports leagues, the NHL has a ready-made institution for containment—the league office—that gives players financial incentives to stay within acceptable boundaries. So now let's look at a tougher case for containment: the honor codes of urban gangs and of the police tasked with preventing violent crime.

As we learned in Chapter Four, honor norms typically emerge in environments with scarce resources and a lack of reliable third-party enforcement. These conditions are present in many inner-city neighborhoods, and the young men and women turn to honor to adapt to them. David Kennedy, the director of the Center of Crime Control at the John Jay College of Criminal Justice, sums up their attitudes:

> It is a community where men will kill for their brothers, die for their brothers, where being a thug is a good and honorable thing, where thug love means having your brothers' backs, no matter what the cost. It is a world in which young men stand against a powerful, malevolent world and say to themselves and to each other, Prison's no big thing; I'm going to be dead by the time I'm twenty-five, so nothing really matters; if a man is disrespected, he has to return violence or he's not a man; the enemy of my friend is my enemy.

Honor values don't need to be imposed in these communities. The norms for toughness, courage, loyalty, and collective punishment are already in place. What's missing, tragically, is the containment.

It's easy to see why. Extreme poverty makes people desperate, hopeless, and angry. "I didn't eat this morning, I'm wearing my niece's clothes," says community activist Ameena Matthews, describing the mind-set. "I just was violated by my mom's boyfriend. I go to school and here comes someone that bumps into me and don't say excuse me. You hit zero to rage within thirty seconds. And you act out." A destructive sense of fatalism pervades these communities, which removes all incentive to stay within the boundaries of larger society. Compounding the problem is the absence of elders with cooler heads and a better understanding of the consequences of violence. Most are in prison, or dead, or they've left the neighborhoods in search of a better life for their families.

By far the greatest obstacle to containing honor in these environments is the presence of guns. The leading cause of death among young black males is getting shot, resulting in a literal arms race among gang members and other community members. Both of honor's dangers are present: escalation and the content of honor norms. The content of honor norms, such as "stand up for yourself and your crew" and "don't get disrespected," is not the problem, though. In other contexts, such norms function perfectly well. The problem is the norms concerning *how* to stand up for yourself and your crew—specifically in relation to guns and violence.

The problems are easy enough to identify, but the solutions are not. The tough prison policies of the past four decades have produced mass incarceration but no lasting decrease in violence within the communities. Why? Because tough prison policies don't change community norms about guns. "Punishment doesn't drive behavior," says epidemiologist Gary Slutkin. "Copying and modeling and the social expectations of your peers is what drives your behavior." Sustained progress in the fight against gun violence, according to the 2015 *Annual Review of Public Health,* "requires changing the social norms that perpetuate violence and the use of guns."

In the past two decades, two movements have emerged that aim to do just that: change social norms about gun violence. Confusingly, they both started out with the same name—Ceasefire—and both have since changed their names to avoid getting conflated. The more recent program was developed by Gary Slutkin and now goes by the name Cure Violence. Tio Hardiman was the first to implement Slutkin's model, creating the "Violence Interrupters" program in Chicago in 2004. (The program, Hardiman, and three other staff members were the subject of Steve James's documentary *The Interrupters.*) Hardiman and Slutkin recruited former and current gang leaders from all over Chicago for the program in the belief that only people who were "in the life" have the credibility to defuse the tempers and emotions that cause the violence. It's a wise tactic. Respected older community members are essential for changing norms in honor cultures. The Cure Violence staff identifies conflicts that threaten to explode in the surrounding communities and then sends the former gang leaders—the "violence interrupters"—to mediate between the disputants. "The interrupters have to deal with how to get someone to save face," says Slutkin. "In other words, how do you not do a shooting if someone has insulted you, if all of your friends are expecting you to do that?... In fact, what our interrupters do is put social pressure in the other direction."

It's a delicate and difficult task because of the strong norms of violent revenge in the community. In the *New York Times Magazine* article that inspired the film, Alex Kotlowitz interviewed a man named Martin Torres whose nephew had been murdered in Chicago. He took a bus from Austin, Texas, to Chicago, plotting a revenge murder before the violence interrupters persuaded him to hold back. "I felt like a punk," he tells Kotlowitz. "'I feel shameful.' [Torres] said he had sought revenge for people who weren't related to him—'people who weren't even no blood to me.' But he held back in the case of his nephew. 'I still struggle with it.... Something made me do what [violence interrupter] Zale asked me to do,' Torres said later, looking more puzzled than comforted. 'Which is respect my brother's wishes.'" Slutkin explains the puzzlement as cognitive dissonance. "Before Zale walked up to him, this guy was holding only one thought," Slutkin says. "So you want to put another thought in his head. *It turns out talking about family* is what really makes a difference."

In addition to mediating violent conflicts, Cure Violence employs outreach workers to further the long-term goals of bettering the communities. Even for these jobs, they try to find workers who are known to the community—credible and respected, sometimes because of their criminal history. The outreach workers connect the community members with opportunities for jobs, housing, recreational activities, and education. The goal is to give high-risk young men and women hope for a better life and, in doing so, shift the incentives and attitudes about violence.

A controversial aspect of Cure Violence is that the violence interrupters don't collaborate with local law enforcement. Since cooperating with police is against the code of the street, the interrupters would lose the credibility they need to mediate the conflicts. This approach is consistent with research on effective mediation. Effective settlement agents, writes sociologist Mark Cooney, "must be slightly higher in status and relatively intimate with the principals... regardless of whether they are state officials, private individuals, or a hybrid of both." One of the great promises of community policing is that it can build relationships between law enforcement and the neighborhoods they patrol, with officers acting more like hockey officials, accepted as part of the community. As it stands, however, the gangs and even the law-abiding citizens in these neighborhoods view the police (often with good reason) as hostile outsiders.

When implemented, Cure Violence has met with considerable success, with reductions of 41 percent to 70 percent in shootings and killings in Chicago, 20 percent in New York City, as well as a startling 73 percent drop in San Pedro Sula, Honduras. A John Hopkins study found more mixed results in Baltimore. They confirmed a 56 percent reduction in homicides and a 34 percent reduction in nonfatal shootings. But another study found no significant differences in norm change between the Cure Violence neighborhoods and a control group. However, a second wave of surveys found greater awareness of community mobilization against gun violence.

The second violence prevention program is one I discussed briefly in Chapter Three. It was developed in Boston by David Kennedy under the name "Operation Ceasefire." The program produced the "Boston Miracle," a stunning reduction in homicides in the mid-1990s. (Kennedy's excellent book, *Don't Shoot*, describes his efforts in lively detail.) The group is now known as Group Violence Intervention. Like Cure Violence, GVI employs street outreach workers to contact high-risk gang members and prevent retaliatory shootings. And like Cure Violence, GVI emphasizes informal social control within communities and groups. The central difference between the two programs is that GVI does collaborate with law enforcement in order to create credible deterrence against shootings. Whereas Cure Violence offers only carrots to reduce violence, GVI uses both carrots and sticks.

Kennedy's model is based on several core principles. The first is that serious acts of violence in urban neighborhoods are perpetuated by a very small number of young men. "Not an entire generation," writes Kennedy, "not everybody in the hot neighborhoods, not all the young black men. Not everybody exposed to violent video games or rap. Not everybody from a single-parent family.... Not everybody who'd been disrespected. Hardly anyone, in fact.... [M]ost gang members never killed anyone. Most years, most gangs never killed anyone." The small number of truly violent actors leads Kennedy to believe that gun violence is a manageable problem. Reducing rates of violence doesn't require solving all the ills of society, such as poor education, lack of jobs, single-parent households, and institutionalized racism. While we have plenty of other moral reasons to address these ills, we shouldn't use them as an excuse for inaction or despair about gun violence.

Kennedy's second principle is that almost all gang members and at-risk youth are rational. They're not the nihilistic, sociopathic superpredators the media and pop culture often portray them to be. They will refrain from violent behavior when it's in their interest. Indeed, most of them *want* to do so. So why do they stockpile guns and start long-running murderous beefs? For reasons like those that Ameena Mathews states above: They're living in difficult, abusive, often humiliating home environments. They go to terrible schools with no resources and teachers who treat them like prisoners. Gangs give them a place to gather, friends and enemies, a shared purpose, protection, and a pathway to respect. "They do terrible things to protect themselves, they have terrible norms and values pressed upon them," Kennedy writes.

> They may act accordingly but it doesn't mean they like it. They're actually looking for a way out.... Even the gang kids are scared to death.... The fear, the group said, makes them join gangs, it makes them get guns, it makes them carry guns, it makes them use violence to show they shouldn't be messed with. The fear, the group said, had become an independent force. It was both an outcome of and an input into the street craziness, a positive feedback loop.

If you grew up in a safe neighborhood like I did, it can be hard to relate to these sentiments. But the fear these young men and women experience is completely rational.

Kennedy's third core principle is that people in this community lack information about the consequences of gun violence. The sentencing process—federal, state, youth versus adult—is mysterious for legal professionals, never mind teenagers. The gang members have no idea how much time they would spend in prison for gun crimes, nor what their odds were of getting caught.

Together, these principles led Kennedy and his group in Boston to implement a policy of *focused and credible deterrence*. "Law enforcement, criminal justice, is a massive, one-size-fits-all architecture," Kennedy writes. It tells them, don't be in a gang, don't commit crimes, don't sell drugs or carry weapons, don't drink unless you're twenty-one, go back to school, get a job—too many lines in the sand to credibly enforce. The strategy of Kennedy's group, by contrast, was customized, particular, highly specific: "Don't shoot." Stop the gun violence.

Crucially, GVI aims their deterrence at the level of the group. The guiding belief is that informal social control—"shame, conscience, guilt, what your friends think, what your mom thinks, what your community thinks"—means more to high-risk youths than the formal social control of police, trials, and possible sentences. To that end, GVI employs a tactic familiar to all honor cultures: collective responsibility. The goal is to give gang members reasons to police their own. Working with police, the group arranges meetings in the targeted communities where they speak to gang leaders and gang members face-to-face. This isn't a sting, they say—we're giving you information that's important to you. Gang violence is a federal matter now. Anyone caught shooting is going to do serious time. But it won't just be he who suffers: "We'll focus on everyone in the gang. We'll arrest drug dealers and shut the markets down. We'll serve warrants. We'll call in probation and parole. Nobody's going to smoke a joint or drink in public, nobody's going to have any fun. We'll talk to the judges and make sure they know what's going on. We'll talk to your parents. It's up to you whether you get this attention."

Essentially, GVI employs a less radical version of "Hamsterdam"—Lieutenant Bunny Colvin's plan in the great TV series *The Wire* to legalize drugs in a certain area of Baltimore in exchange for no violence. Kennedy's group doesn't offer to legalize drugs. Rather, they promise to devote far more police attention to the drug dealing of violent gangs and (by implication) less attention to the nonviolent ones. And they keep that promise.

Like Cure Violence, GVI has met with great success when implemented properly, with significant reductions in violent crimes and shooting-related incidents. The strategy has been effective for several reasons. It gives the gang members an excuse to refrain from violent behavior—which almost all of them want to do anyway—without signaling weakness. It gives gangs incentives to police their own violent actors, since the gang's financial future depends on it. And because *all* the gangs share an interest in doing business without massive police interference, GVI's deal offers gangs and individuals caught up in beefs an "honorable exit" from the violence.

The GVI program also treats the community with respect. The officers treat them as rational agents, not sociopaths—something many of them rarely get to experience, especially from police. And finally, the program broadens the circle of caring, good people in the community, all of whom want safer neighborhoods and better lives for the citizens. In Boston, Kennedy writes:

> We had cops acting like social workers and trying to get gang members jobs, outreach workers acting like cops and bringing law enforcement to bear, street ministers acting like prosecutors and fingering impact players, prosecutors organizing job programs, gang members turning in other gang members, neighborhood people reinforcing the law enforcement messages.... The racial code talk is gone.... If this group says black kids are killing each other and it has to stop, it doesn't really mean that it thinks the black family is collapsing, or that black kids are sociopaths, or that the community is hollow and corrupt. It means that black kids are killing each other and it has to stop.

This is how honor groups deal with each other. Straightforward, honest, respectful. It is a model example of containing rather than rejecting honor, mining its virtues, harnessing its motivational resources, while at the same time limiting its excesses.

"Aggression into Art": The World of Battle Rap

The two programs described above are designed to contain the violence and aggression within the honor cultures of inner-city gang life. My third example of well-functioning honor seeks not only to contain aggression but also to harness and direct it toward positive (and legal) ends. Harnessing aggression is crucial to succeed in the growing community of battle rap. Battling has been around since the beginning of hip-hop, but more recently formal leagues have formed to showcase the best and most popular artists. Rules vary according to the leagues and events, but the basic setup is as follows. Two rappers—usually men, sometimes women—stand face-to-face, surrounded by their respective crews and a large crowd of onlookers. Battles usually last three rounds, and in each round the rapper tries to "outwit, outflow, and outdis" his opponent. In the early days, battles were mostly improvised, and rappers were judged by how well they could think, and rhyme, on their feet. In most modern league battles, however, rappers prepare their verses in advance and throw in a few spontaneous rhymes when inspiration strikes. The verses typically alternate between dissing opponents and boasting about the rapper's own prowess—often exaggerated for comic effect.

When you watch a battle for the first time, you might think it's dangerous and unstable. But the disses and violent boasts are all part of game, part of this expressive art form that grew out of the African American insult game called "the dozens," where the goal is to come up with the best insult for your opponent's mother. Since most rappers come from tough neighborhoods, many boasts involve selling drugs, shooting, killing, robbing, pimping, and sex—often with their opponents' girlfriends and moms.

Like most honor frameworks, battle rap offers opportunities for individual achievement within a communal framework. Rappers don't just boast about themselves; they celebrate their crew, neighborhood, city, tradition, and heritage. Competitions are open to people from all races and cultural backgrounds—black, Asian, Italian, Hispanic, Jews—and the slurs fly at a hilarious and rapid pace. These are not microaggressions either, or even macroaggressions— they're whatever is above macro. Out of context, they would seem bigoted and almost cruel. But talent and wit can win over almost any crowd, and the truth is that the battles celebrate diversity and cultural pride in ways that diversity seminars and workshops never could.

Hip-hop has plenty of critics and scolds who complain about the glorification of violence and crime in rap. They're not wrong about the glorification, but what they often miss are the opportunities for positive norm change—not just about guns, but about gang life in general. Take, for example, Loaded Lux's legendary final round in his 2012 Summer Slam battle against Calicoe. Calicoe had spent his rounds establishing his reputation as a hard Detroit gangster. Calicoe's father had been one of the leaders of Detroit's Black Mafia Family in the late '80s, which gave Calicoe some instant credibility. Loaded Lux started his final round by deflating some of Calicoe's pretensions, a common battle strategy. On a big screen behind him, Lux showed a PowerPoint of an Instagram photo Calicoe posted of swimming naked with some friends, saying, "So that's how Detroit gangstas do? / Skinny-dippin' gone wild?" This was standard stuff, but it earned big laughs from his home crowd in New York. But then Lux's round takes a more serious turn. As hip-hop scholar Shiva Mavima describes it, Lux "condemns the destructive virtues embodied by gang life, and questions why Calico's father had

not gotten a '9–5' like a responsible parent would instead of ped-
dling drugs in the community and being arrested for much of Calicoe's life." Lux returns repeatedly to the refrain "your pops wasn't no
gangsta, he was just another lost nigga" and goes on to praise the
"real gangsters," the historic heroes of the black community, such as
Marcus Garvey, Nat Turner, and Harriet Tubman, who "was more
of a man than [Calicoe's] father would ever be." To this day, many
rappers and battle aficionados calls Lux's final round the best battle round of all time. P-Diddy had attended, and Jay Z tweeted out
links to the battle along with the line "He gon' get this work!" that
Loaded Lux used repeatedly to get the rowdy crowd to calm down
so he could continue his verse. The canonization of verses like Lux's,
writes Mavima, reflects the value of communal responsibility in
black culture. In an interview, Mavima asked rapper Pharaoh Soul
to name the best battle he had seen. Pharoah Soul singled out a battle in which Remy D called out his opponent, T-Dubb, for his unre-
lenting emphasis on gunplay in battles: "As Pharaoh Soul explained
to me, 'he stopped talking about what guns do, and started talking
about what guns do,' that is, instead of focusing on the glamorized
use of guns as an extension of one's masculinity, and described how
violence had been destructive to the hood: 'I don't respect niggas living your life standards / coz when you categorize the victims your
type adds up / they usually classified as innocent bystanders.'"

It's true that these verses are more the exception than the rule—
most battles have plenty of references to violence and crime. For one
thing, sanctimony and moralistic sermonizing don't lead to effective

norm change. For another, expressing violent impulses is part of the skill of battling—where the "aggression into art" mantra becomes more than just a myth that "captured the liberal imagination." And crucially for the theme of this chapter (containment!), the aggression in battle rap is confined to words and contained within the arena of competition. No fights allowed. On very rare occasions, an insult might touch a nerve, and a punch gets thrown. But the fight is immediately broken up, and it usually leads to a suspension from the league. When the rounds are over, battlers usually hug or shake hands, no matter how vicious the attacks were during the battle. Nobody wants to get suspended; nobody wants to lose money and status (and open themselves up for future attacks). Like the B-boy break-dancing battles in the '70s and '80s, rap battles are effective opportunities for poor kids of all races and creeds to gain status, honor, and for some even a steady income, all through nonviolent means.

Lessons and Challenges

These are just a few examples of well-contained honor; there are plenty of others: poetry slams, school team sports, backyard bare-knuckled fighting leagues (such as those featured in the documentary *Dawg Fight*), and of course restorative justice, an honorable and contained means of resolving conflicts. Just before my deadline for turning in the book, I came across a new Chicago program that in one year reduced violent-crime arrests by 50 percent and improved high school graduation rates (19 percent) among young men. It's called BAM—"Becoming a Man"—and its six core values epitomize the idea of contained honor that I've tried to flesh out in this chapter and throughout the book. The values are *integrity* ("My values equal my actions; I am a man of my word"), *accountability* ("I am responsible for the consequences of my actions whether intended or unintended; I take ownership for what I do and avoid projecting blame"), *positive anger expression* ("I learn that anger is a normal emotion that needs to be expressed; how I express my anger is a choice, whether as a savage or as a warrior"), *self-determination* ("I pursue my goals in the face of adversity"), *respect for womanhood* ("I am more mindful and respectful in how I interact with women; I strive to be a self-liberator and not an oppressor"), and *visionary goal setting* ("I create a vision for myself, for who I am, and how I want to be seen in the world; I create a vision that is focused on making my community and the world a better place").

If you've come this far in the book, you'll recognize BAM's core values as central to most honor groups. Recall from Chapter One, for example, that accountability for both intended and unintended actions is far more prevalent in honor cultures than dignity cultures, which often have a strong control condition for responsibility. BAM's values also illustrate key elements of containment. Their goal isn't to eliminate anger but to control it (as warriors learn to control anger). And since mistreatment of women is all too common in urban neighborhoods and honor cultures in general, BAM's core values insist upon treating women with greater respect. (This recalls one of the fifty-six elements of the Bushido Samurai code: "The warrior who strikes his wife is a coward.")

Contained honor comes in too many forms to give a precise account of what the features have in common. But the following are some elements that are typical of well-functioning contained honor systems. The first is *flexibility, with an emphasis on moral character building.* Honor groups are skeptical of one-size-fits-all solutions. They mistrust idealized solutions and exceptionless general principles, showing a preference for flexible, focused, particularized engagement. Again, we can turn to the BAM program for an excellent illustration. BAM requires students to meet four times a month, and a trained counselor leads students in discussions about personal challenges in their own lives. They learn a variety of practices and activities—like meditation and archery—that help them regulate and control their emotions and channel their energy toward productive goals. The counselors avoid telling youth what is the "right" and "wrong" thing to do, which is different from many moral values programs:

> For that matter, BAM never teaches youth not to get angry, or even that they should never fight—because the program providers realize youth are growing up in difficult neighborhood environments where they will be challenged and sometimes need to fight back. Providers tell youth "if you fight be sure it's only when you have to," and report that while most youth wind up fighting less, some stand up to challenges more often due to BAM.

Analysts trace the success of BAM in part to this shift from moral rules to moral character, which allows for greater flexibility in addressing the particular challenges the young men face.

Well-functioning honor communities also tend to be *small and relatively egalitarian*. People in honor groups need to know each other and be generally aware of the group members' behavior. Too much anonymity makes it difficult to acquire reputations and to care about the reputation you have.

The communities should also feature *a good mix of youth and experience*. Younger group members bring passion, energy, and new ideas. Elders can relate the benefits of experience and rein in the excesses of youth. All of the examples in this chapter—the NHL, Cure Violence, GVI, the rap-battle community, and BAM—have elders within the community who are respected by the youth. In addition, keeping the community relatively small makes it easier for members to develop strong social ties, strong relationships, and a positive form of group identification.

Another element these communities have in common is *personalized conflict resolution and skilled mediators*. Most honor cultures have a norm for handling your own business when it comes to conflict. When possible, people should address disputes within the group directly—with trusted mediators available to step in when necessary. The mediators should be members of the community. But they shouldn't have too close a relationship to either party. Recall sociologist Mark Cooney's claim that the best peacemakers are neither too low nor too high in status relative to the principals. Too low and they won't command the respect of the disputant. Too high, Cooney writes, and they'll have "a strong tendency to be moralistic," eschew "consultation, compromise, and conciliation in favor of control, commands, and coercion." Disputants in conflicts don't like moralistic mediators and will often turn their backs on mediation efforts if they demonstrate moralistic attitudes.

Finally, well-contained honor cultures typically flourish in environments in which *basic needs are met*. Honor's violent side is much harder to contain when people are desperate or hopeless. Accordingly, honor groups function best when the needs for food, clothing, shelter, education, and employment are satisfied. For these reasons, the best programs devote resources and attention to community outreach that helps individuals meet these basic requirements.

This list of elements isn't exhaustive, and many well-functioning honor cultures don't have all of them. Unfortunately, these elements aren't sufficient either for honor communities to flourish. Even the most successful honor frameworks face tough obstacles in modern society. Both the Cure Violence and the Group Violence Intervention programs, for example, have struggled to gain widespread implementation despite overwhelming evidence that they reduce gun violence and other violent crimes. Often this is for political reasons. Existing institutions feel threatened. Turf wars are rampant. Not from the gangs, but from the various agencies that deal with crime. Even in Boston, where GVI's success was celebrated and unambiguous, the program didn't last. The institutions wouldn't cooperate. As street worker Teny Gross put it in an op-ed for the *Boston Globe*:

> There was glory enough for everybody, but the cooperation
> turned to competition and control. There is no polite way to say
> it: Boston's regression into its old territorial self has translated
> directly into death. A decade ago a young man in Dorchester told

me, "You adults are the real gang members, easy to feel slighted, fighting petty beefs, vying for attention and credit." It is the beefs on the streets that get the headlines. But the beefs in the offices and agencies are now equally to blame for what is happening.

Resistance is also born out of ignorance. The best-intentioned people are often reluctant to implement an honor framework simply because they don't know how it really functions. Voters who know very little about Cure Violence and GVI have the impression that it's soft on crime—"hug-a-thug," as right-wing op-ed columnists have referred to it. The same goes for restorative justice programs. When people hear about them in the abstract, they sound touchy-feely, naive, Pollyannaish—hippie justice, the "hug-it-out" approach to justice (what do people have against hugs anyway?). Watching or experiencing concrete cases, however, leads people to almost the opposite impression. To fully appreciate the value of honor systems, you have to experience them firsthand—or at least witness them in action. But because honor systems are insular by nature, outsiders often have difficulty understanding or relating to them. Honor's defenders must find creative forms of outreach that present a more personal and vivid portrait of how it works.

Honor's defenders face theoretical challenges as well. The dominant ethical theories since the Enlightenment are abstract, idealized, systematic, foundational, and universalizable. Honor has none of these attributes. Honor norms are local, not universal. They are complex, messy, unsystematic, at times even incoherent. Most important, honor is a thoroughly nonideal form of value.

Dignity-based theories, or utilitarian theories, can produce utopian ideals under perfect conditions. True, conditions are far from perfect in the real world. Moral injustice pervades our criminal justice system, for example; nobody denies that. But the mere prospect of an ideal justice system with no bias or error, where all criminals receive punishments in precise accordance with their just deserts, is hard to resist. Though practically unattainable, the prospect prevents ethicists from questioning the foundations of the status quo. At least it *aims* for an ideal, even if it can't ever approach it in practice. Honor doesn't strive for perfection and often comes in the form of an "unfinished alternative" or a work in progress.

The allure of perfection is strong, however, and it can get in the way of better but nonideal alternatives. Honor groups must convince skeptics to compare their approaches with actual rather than idealized options. Worried about racial bias within restorative justice programs? It's a legitimate concern, but compare how it works in practice with the racial bias in our current system *as it exists*, not as it is supposed to exist. And if restorative justice fares better, then institute it and work to improve this aspect of its approach. Concerned about inconsistent enforcement of drug laws under Group Violence Intervention policies? Fair enough, but compare that moral cost to the costs of higher homicide rates and the abiding mistrust and hostility toward police. Compare it to the costs of zero-tolerance or three-strikes-and-you're-out policies, all of which were instituted in the name of consistency in sentencing. And so on, down the line. Well-contained honor-oriented approaches may have inherent defects, yet still be morally preferable by a mile to systematic and idealized approaches that could achieve perfection "in principle." The old saying "Don't let the perfect get in the way of the good" is worth taking very seriously here. If we allow honor to work its magic, while limiting its excesses, we can make actual rather than theoretical progress.

EPILOGUE

The specter of W. W. Beauchamp has haunted me throughout the writing of this book. Beauchamp is a side character in Clint Eastwood's masterpiece *Unforgiven*, the dime-store author who chronicles the adventures of gunslingers in the Old West. He swears by the accuracy of his accounts, but it's clear from the outset that Beauchamp romanticizes his subjects, depicting them as honor-bound knights when they're in fact brutal and merciless killers. In the film, Beauchamp accompanies British bounty hunter English Bob on his way to the town of Little Whiskey. Beauchamp is writing Bob's biography, "The Duke of Death." What happens to English Bob is mostly unconnected to the main narrative, but it perfectly distills the movie's themes. As soon as Bob and Beauchamp roll into town, Sheriff Little Bill takes away his guns and gives him a brutal beating in front of the townspeople. Beauchamp pees his pants. Little Bill then throws Bob in the town jail and unravels the myth of English Bob completely. As he exits the town the next day, Bob is a raving lunatic, shouting insults at America from the back of a horse carriage. Beauchamp, far from chastened, just changes the subject of his biography from Bob to Little Bill, eager to get started on a new romantic myth.

So I've approached this four-year project holding W. W. Beauchamp as my cautionary tale, doing my best to separate the romance of honor cultures from the reality. In the meantime, Donald Trump became president, and white nationalist, neofascist, neo-Nazi groups have gained national attention. Thankfully, they seldom mention the word *honor*, and *white people* is far too diffuse and amorphous to count as anything like an honor group. But the white nationalists do use rhetoric that isn't too far off from the language I've employed to describe honor communities. They bemoan the atomization of white society. They portray themselves as victims of multicultural oppression, humiliated by a powerful and politically correct State. To combat this "oppression," they urge white people to embrace their white identity. They've embraced a movement, identitarianism, with origins in Far Right neofascist groups in France, Germany, and Scandinavia. This past weekend (August 11–13, 2017), as I am writing this, the groups united in Charlottesville, Virginia, to protest against the removal of a Confederate statue. The protest turned violent. It was an eye-opening event for many Americans, including me, who didn't quite realize the extent of their abhorrent racist ideology. It's scary stuff, and it would be naive to think there won't be more incidents like this between now and this book's publication.

As a consequence, tribal value systems, including honor, are of even lower repute among classical liberals and moderate conservatives than they were when I began this project. Proponents of

Western liberalism, Enlightenment values, and the culture of dignity regard the past few years as vindication. About a month before this book is scheduled to be published, Steven Pinker's new book, *Enlightenment NOW*, will come out. I haven't seen a draft, but I'm willing to bet that honor values will attract some more of his ire. And that's fine. Like any value system, honor should be subjected to serious critical scrutiny. Moreover, the past few years *should* make us more appreciative of the morality of dignity and its focus on equality and respect for human rights.

At the same time, there's a smugness to the most triumphalist champions of liberalism, an elitist "let-them-eat-dignity" quality, that ignores or undervalues the serious problems of modern life, especially for the least educated and least fortunate. The resurgence of Far Right nationalism in the United States and Western Europe has exposed the inherent weaknesses and vulnerabilities of our culture of dignity. These movements didn't emerge out of nowhere. Human beings crave communal connections; they crave purpose and meaning and seek to identify with movements, causes, and groups. This is a well-documented fact of human psychology. The policies and social structure of dignity cultures place all the moral emphasis on the individual, which, along with the depersonalizing forces of industrialization, has left many people feeling lost, alienated, humiliated, and seething with resentment. That void, the lack of meaning, community, and forms of identification, will get filled somehow. The question is how it gets filled, what we identify with, how we derive meaning and purpose from our lives. Liberal morality by design doesn't give positive answers to these questions; it gives us the freedom to answer them in our own way. But that's not enough. As I hope I've demonstrated throughout the book, honor offers flexible and psychologically realistic frameworks that can satisfy these deep human needs. Yes, we need to be careful about honor's darker aspects, but we should embrace the many positive manifestations that stay within the broad boundaries of rights-based morality.

ACKNOWLEDGMENTS

As I was developing my idea for a book, I called psychologist and prolific author Paul Bloom for advice. He listened to my pitch and with his usual empathetic (yes empathetic!) tact, steered me in a different direction. "It's funny," Paul said, "based on our conversations, I would have thought you'd be writing a book on honor." And that was that. So thanks to Paul for reminding me to write the book I was supposed to write.

My agent, Russell Weinberg, worked with me over two years developing the proposal and nailing down the argument. I wanted to give up on the project many times in the earlier part of the process, and Russell encouraged me to keep trying. I'm also grateful to Russell for reading several drafts of the book and helping me find my voice.

Thanks to T.J. Kelleher, editor at Basic Books, for offering me the contract and for his valuable editing suggestions throughout the process. I'm grateful to Leah Stecher, also an editor at Basic Books, for her detailed notes on an early draft of the manuscript. Thanks to everyone at Basic Books for marshaling the book through to publication.

I've spent countless hours talking to David Pizarro about honor, revenge, and restorative justice. True, it was on our podcast *Very Bad Wizards*, and even now, after five years, he still doesn't fully appreciate the virtues of restorative justice. I'll never give up, though, and I'm grateful to David for his challenges, good humor, and encouragement.

Big thanks to the graduate students in my seminar on honor in the fall of 2014. Our discussions throughout the semester were invaluable as I formed the argument for this book. Special thanks to Valerie Soon (now at Duke); I've incorporated several of her insights about honor's value for battling oppression in Chapter Four. Thanks also to David Sommers, Vida Yao, and Justin Coates for reading drafts of the manuscript and offering helpful suggestions to improve it.

Thanks to the University of Houston for giving me a semester leave to work on this project. I'm especially grateful to David Phillips (Philosophy Department chair) and Bill Monroe (dean of the Honors College) for being flexible with my schedule, allowing me the time to finish this project.

Over the past dozen years, I've had many valuable conversations about honor and responsibility, all of which have helped to shaped my views. I'm sure this list isn't exhaustive (and I apologize to anyone I left out), but thanks to William Ian Miller, Anthony Appiah, Fiery Cushman, John Doris, Shaun Nichols, David Shoemaker, John Bickle, Nancy Sherman, Steve Stich, Steve

Burke, Dan Demetriou, Ron Mallon, Hagop Sarkissian, Kim Meyer, Gabriela Maya, Cameron Bruckner, Michael McKenna, Joe Henrich, Liane Young, Josh Greene, Josh Knobe, Felipe de Brigard, Eddy Nahmias, Pavel Nitchovski, Dan Weiner, and Eddie Guzelian.

My wife, Jennifer Sommers, has read several drafts of this book and helped to shape it more than anyone else. Many of the book's virtues (and all its defects) are due to her influence. I'm so grateful to Jen and my daughter, Eliza, for their loving, good-humored support, for making our small house a pleasant place to work and a wonderful place to stop working. Finally, thanks to my dogs, Charlie and Omar, for keeping me company as I wrote the book. They offered unwavering enthusiasm even during the darkest periods of the writing process.

NOTES

PROLOGUE

3   **"fetishisized virtues such as":** Steven Pinker, *The Better Angels of Our Nature: A History of Violence and Humanity*, 183.

3   **honor is hardly mentioned in the contemporary:** Exceptions include work by Anthony Appiah, Anthony Cunningham, Dan Demetriou, Peter Olsthoorn, Laurie Johnson, Sharon Krause, and Shannon French.

3   **"exiled to some philosophical St. Helena":** Anthony Appiah, *The Honor Code: How Moral Revolutions Happen*, loc. 2375, Kindle.

3   **"strange commodity that exists":** Pinker, *Better Angels of Our Nature*, 23.

6   **WEIRD (Western, educated, industrialized, rich, and democratic) societies:** Anthropologist Joe Henrich and colleagues coined the acronym WEIRD to denote societies in the modern West that have these attitudes about fairness, justice, and other ethical and political views. See Joe Henrich et al., *Foundations of Human Sociality: Economic Experiments and Ethnographic Evidence from Fifteen Small-Scale Societies* and "The Weirdest People in the World?"

CHAPTER ONE

16 **"doing his best to disappear in plain sight":** Jason Turbow and Michael Duca, *The Baseball Codes: Beanballs, Sign Stealing, and Bench-Clearing Brawls—the Unwritten Rules of America's Pastime*, 113. Turbow and Duca's book is chock-full of entertaining stories about baseball's unwritten honor codes.

16 **"We will not tolerate the guys":** Ibid., 112.

17 **helpful distinction between two dimensions of honor:** See Frank Henderson Stewart, *Honor*.

18 **Having horizontal honor is like:** Brett McKay, Art of Manliness (blog), www.artofmanliness.com/2012/10/01/manly-honor-part-i-what-is-honor/.

22 **"In an honor based culture":** William Ian Miller, *Humiliation, and Other Essays on Honor, Social Discomfort, and Violence*, 116.

24 **your virtues:** The concept of "virtue" has acquired a fair amount of philosophical and political baggage. Throughout I'll use the word *virtue* in its broadest sense, meaning "admirable character traits."

24 **"If my name ever goes down":** See Sharon R. Krause, *Liberalism with Honor*, 135.

26 **"implies that identity is essentially independent":** Peter Berger, "On the Obsolescence of the Concept of Honor," 177.

26 **"The implicit sociology [of dignity]":** Ibid.

27 **"to avoid being bothered decent and street youths alike":** Elijah Anderson, *Code of the Street: Decency, Violence, and the Moral Life of the Inner City*, 106.

27 **"With the right amount of respect":** Ibid., 33.

29 **"The crusher who becomes a rusher":** Ross Bernstein, *The Code: The Unwritten Rules of Fighting and Retaliation in the NHL*, loc. 1985, Kindle.

29 **"As kids we all had visions of being the guy":** Ibid., 1821.

31 **If you travel to Iran:** See www.bbc.com/travel/story/20161104-the-persian-art-of-etiquette.

33 **"With subtle remarks on lukewarm tea":** Andrew Shryock, "The New Jordanian Hospitality: House, Host, and Guest in the Culture of Public Display, 36."

34 **"the supreme ethical category":** Ismail Kadare, *Broken April*, 76.

34 **It is a striking and somewhat puzzling fact:** Some theories suggest that hospitality norms are for ensuring the possibility of travel among potentially hostile communities and groups. Guests proposing peace treaties or bringing goods for trade had to be protected from harm and theft. In addition, since forms of travel were much slower, travelers had to make several stops before arriving at their destination. See, for example, https://minerva.union.edu/ wareht/gkcultur/guide/8/web1.html. Although there is plenty of research on hospitality norms in honor cultures, there is very little scholarly work on the origin and function of these norms.

35 **"honor means 'don't tread on me'":** W. Miller, *Humiliation*, 84.

35 **"is someone willing to acknowledge":** Bill Bonanno, *Bound by Honor: A Mafioso's Story*, xvi.

36 **"follows no norms of conduct":** Orit Kamir, "Honor and Dignity Cultures: The Case of *Kavod* (Honor) and *Kvod Ha-adam* (Dignity) in Israeli Society and Law," 16.

37 **"no one steps up and demands justice":** Bonanno, *Bound by Honor*, xvi.

37 **This aversion to third-party involvement:** See Laura Blumenfeld, *Revenge: A Story of Hope*.

38 **"revealed very sharply in the inability":** Berger, "On the Obsolescence of the Concept of Honor," 172.

38 **"were fighting not for money":** Pinker, *Better Angels of Our Nature*, 23.

39 **"revulsion from sexual activity":** J. K. Campbell, "Honour and the Devil," 146.

39 **"always implicates the honor of the men":** Ibid.

39 **"hardly the downtrodden, submissive and self-effacing beings":** Jill Dubisch, *Gender & Power in Rural Greece*, 10.

40 "What about an honor culture like my saga Iceland guys": Tamler
    Sommers, *A Very Bad Wizard: Morality Behind the Curtain*, 101.

40 "It's just a complex social psychological fact": Ibid., 122.

42 "the ethos of honor is fundamentally opposed": Pierre Bourdieu,
    *Algeria, 1960: The Disenchantment of the World, The Sense of Honour,
    The Kabyle House or the World Reversed*, 129.

42 "They are in no way capable": Ibid.

43 "What Japan, and indeed portions of the Middle East": Gary S.
    Gregg, *The Middle East: A Cultural Psychology*, 30.

CHAPTER TWO

49 the Western media "painted the bullseye": Allahpundit, "Charlie
    Hebdo Editor Warns Western Media: 'We Can't Be the Only Ones
    to Stand up for These Values,'" *Hot Air*, May 4, 2015, hotair.com/
    archives/2015/05/04/charlie-hebdo-editor-warns-western-media
    -we-cant-be-the-only-ones-to-stand-up-for-these-values/.

49 consequences beyond the paper's own journalistic failures: The
    hashtag #spreadtherisk went viral afterward in response to the
    refusal of newspapers like the *Times* to publish the cartoons.

50 "an unbreakable commitment to defend": Marcus Luttrell
    and Patrick Robinson, *Lone Survivor: The Eyewitness Account of
    Operation Redwing and the Lost Heroes of SEAL Team 10*, 282–283.

51 "France should remain as it is": Michael Tomasky, "François
    Hollande Shows True Grit on Refugees," *Daily Beast*, November
    19, 2015, www.thedailybeast.com/francois-hollande-shows-true-grit
    -on-refugees.

53 "The annual number of abductions": Pinker, *Better Angels of Our
    Nature*, 446.

54 "As a social scientist": Ryan P. Brown, *Honor Bound: How a Cultural
    Ideal Has Shaped the American Psyche*, loc. 3233–3234, Kindle.

56 Other sources of motivation: See Appiah, *Honor Code*; and
    Sommers, *Very Bad Wizard*.

57 **"I wanted the chance to prove"**: Sebastian Junger, *Tribe*, xiv.

58 **"Only gods and heroes"**: Steven Pressfield, *Gates of Fire: An Epic Novel of the Battle of Thermopylae*, 36–37.

59 **distinguished between two types of social relations**: See Jonathan Haidt and Selin Kesebir, "Morality," for a good analysis of this distinction.

59 **"a circle of men who"**: Joan Aldous et al., "An Exchange Between Durkheim and Tonnies on the Nature of Social Relations, with an Introduction by Joan Aldous," 48–49.

59 **"characterized by a high degree of individualism"**: Robert Nisbet cited in Jonathan Haidt and Jesse Graham, "Planet of the Durkheimians, Where Community, Authority, and Sacredness Are Foundations of Morality."

61 **suicide rates were significantly higher**: The rates were much lower in more integrated groups, for people in large families, for example, and for Jews and Catholics rather than Protestants. See ibid.

61 **rates skyrocket after rapid modernization**: See Roy J. Shephard and Andris Rode, *The Health Consequences of "Modernization": Evidence from Circumpolar Peoples*.

61 **A RAND Corporation study**: See Junger, *Tribe*.

61 **"social cohesiveness, a strong family system"**: John Braithwaite, *Crime, Shame and Reintegration*, loc. 1590–1592, Kindle.

62 **"Show of hands, please"**: David M. Kennedy, *Don't Shoot: One Man, a Street Fellowship, and the End of Violence in Inner-City America*, 126.

65 **WEIRD (Western, educated, industrial, rich, and democratic) people**: See Henrich et al., *Foundations of Human Sociality*.

65 **"We learned the code as kids"**: Bernstein, *The Code*, loc. 40, Kindle.

67 **"When Tomas heard Communists"**: Milan Kundera, *The Unbearable Lightness of Being*, 177. I discuss this case in *Relative Justice: Cultural Diversity, Free Will, and Moral Responsibility* as well.

68 **"bored," "frustrated," "offended," and "disgusted":** See Jennifer Jacquet, *Is Shame Necessary? New Uses for an Old Tool.*

CHAPTER THREE

73 **"It was us who gave the brothers":** J. Gram Slattery, "The Meaning of 'Boston Strong': Opinion," *Harvard Crimson*, April 22, 2014, www.thecrimson.com/article/2014/4/22/meaning-of-boston -strong/.

75 **"Why Was Boston Strong?":** Herman B. Leonard et al., "Why Was Boston Strong? Lessons from the Marathon Bombing," 59.

76 **solidarity was significantly correlated:** James Hawdon et al., "Social Solidarity and Wellbeing After Critical Incidents: Three Cases of Mass Shootings." See also James Hawdon and John Ryan, "Social Relations That Generate and Sustain Solidarity After a Mass Tragedy" and "Social Solidarity Measure," for more detail on the measuring of solidarity.

77 **the groundbreaking *Culture of Honor*:** Richard E. Nisbett and Dov Cohen, *Culture of Honor: The Psychology of Violence in the South.*

78 **All of these features:** See ibid., 4–7. See also Tamler Sommers, *Relative Justice* and "The Two Faces of Revenge: Moral Responsibility and the Culture of Honor," for a detailed account of their view and its implications for collective and individual responsibility.

81 **"For immigrant latchkey kids":** Jeff Chang, *Can't Stop, Won't Stop: A History of the Hip-Hop Generation*, 49.

81 **I came across a documentary:** As of this writing, *Check It* is available to watch only on Louis CK's website, louisck.net. See also Courtland Milloy, "Gay Black Youths Go from Attacked to Attackers," *Washington Post*, September 27, 2011, www .washingtonpost.com/local/gay-black-youths-go-from-attacked-to -attackers/2011/09/27/gIQA2JV52K_story.html?utm_term= .c3c27e17f03a.

83 **"We're all in it together":** Luttrell and Robinson, *Lone Survivor*, 79.

84 **"Your reputation begins right here":** Ibid., 90.

84 **many contemporary theories of human cooperation:** See, for example, Natalie Henrich and Joseph Patrick Henrich, *Why Humans Cooperate: A Cultural and Evolutionary Explanation.*

85 **"Back in England every family":** Chang, *Can't Stop, Won't Stop*, 49.

87 **primary evolutionary function of tribal feuds:** Jacob Black-Michaud, *Cohesive Force: Feud in the Mediterranean and the Middle East*; Christopher Boehm, *Blood Revenge: The Anthropology of Feuding in Montenegro and Other Tribal Societies*; and Joseph Ginat, *Blood Revenge: Family Honor, Mediation, and Outcasting*, provide excellent discussions of how conflicts and feuds can build solidarity. In addition, strong retaliation norms of feuding groups are correlated with strong norms of positive reciprocity, which creates strong bonds of mutual influence and obligation. D. Cohen and J. A. Vandello, "The Paradox of Politeness."

88 **"is all about building team unity":** Bernstein, *The Code*, loc. 1058–1063, Kindle.

88 **sports are one area:** See Martin Van Boekel et al., "Effects of Participation in School Sports on Academic and Social Functioning."

90 **"inner satisfaction, distraction, relief":** Robert Nye, "How the Duel of Honour Promoted Civility and Attenuated Violence in Western Europe," loc. 4956, Kindle. See Nye's essay for an excellent discussion of Simmel's views on conflict.

90 **"the clearer perception and livelier impression":** John Stuart Mill, *On Liberty.*

90 **"there is less honor to respect":** Nils Christie, "Conflicts as Property," 6.

91 **"one of the many cases of lost opportunities":** Ibid., 7.

91 **"dead child's family and the child's accidental killers":** Jared Diamond, *The World Until Yesterday: What Can We Learn from Traditional Societies?*, 84.

92   **"The moral order derives a very special kind"**: Braithwaite, *Crime, Shame and Reintegration*, loc. 1414, Kindle.

93   **the egalitarian codes of an honor group**: See Nye, "How the Duel of Honour Promoted Civility"; Randall Collins, *Violence: A Micro-sociological Theory*; and Ben Merriman, "Duels in the European Novel: Honor, Reputation, and the Limits of a Bourgeois Form."

93   **opposed it on precisely these grounds**: Appiah, *Honor Code*, loc. 538, Kindle.

93   **"inaccurate and weak smoothbore pistols"**: Collins, *Violence: A Micro-sociological Theory*, 218, cited in Merriman, "Duels in the European Novel," 205.

93   **"punched him in the face"**: From Andrew Sharp, "The Miami Dolphins and Everything That Will Never Make Sense."

94   **"not to hurt him physically"**: Anderson, *Code of the Street*, 82.

95   **"They have fought, and, for the moment"**: Ibid., 90.

96   **Equality, incidentally, is itself highly correlated**: See Marii Paskov and Caroline Dewilde, "Income Inequality and Solidarity in Europe"; and Bram Lancee and Herman G. van de Werfhorst, "Income Inequality and Participation: A Comparison of 24 European Countries."

CHAPTER FOUR

100   **Michigan psychologists Richard Nisbett and Dov Cohen**: These experiments and their implications are discussed in Nisbett and Cohen, *Culture of Honor*; and Dov Cohen et al., "Insult, Aggression, and the Southern Culture of Honor: An 'Experimental Ethnography.'"

103   **According to the best evolutionary models**: See Peter J. Richerson and Robert Boyd, *Not by Genes Alone: How Culture Transformed Human Evolution*; and Henrich et al., *Foundations of Human Sociality*.

104   **"the target of the whisperings"**: Jacques Busquet, *Le droit de la vendetta et les paci corses*, 357–358.

104 **"A man slow to kill his enemy"**: Margaret Hasluck, *Unwritten Law in Albania*, 231–232.

105 **"man is more naturally chicken"**: William Ian Miller, *Eye for an Eye*, 96.

105 **"the pretty young girls clustered around"**: Steven Pressfield, "The Warrior Ethos."

105 **"Don't come in here crying"**: Anderson, *Code of the Street*, 70–71.

105 **honor norms can be "sticky"**: See Joseph A. Vandello et al., "U.S. Southern and Northern Differences in Perceptions of Norms About Aggression."

107 **The explosion of the US prison population**: See John F. Pfaff, *Locked In: The True Causes of Mass Incarceration—and How to Achieve Real Reform*.

108 **market exchange**: *Market* is defined broadly—this framework, for example, includes questions about proportionality in punishment— determining the proper punishment for a particular crime. See Alan Page Fiske and Tage Shakti Rai, *Virtuous Violence: Hurting and Killing to Create, Sustain, End, and Honor Social Relationships*; and Rai and Fiske, "Moral Psychology Is Relationship Regulation: Moral Motives for Unity, Hierarchy, Equality, and Proportionality."

109 **"I'd rather die"**: Brown, *Honor Bound*, loc. 2979, Kindle.

110 **"What annoyed me most"**: James Maasdorp, "Zidane's Headbutt 10 Years On: The Hit That Shocked the Football World."

110 **"It's hard to explain"**: Andrew Hussey, "Interview: Zinedine Zidane," *Observer*, April 3, 2004, www.theguardian.com/football/ 2004/apr/04/sport.features.

111 **"Our whole family is deeply saddened"**: Tony Karon, "The Head Butt Furor: A Window on Europe's Identity Crisis."

112 **"I now forgot my roots"**: Krause, *Liberalism with Honor*, 145–146.

113 **"It rekindled in my breast"**: Ibid., 146.

113 **"sacrifice money, reputation, and life"**: Ibid., 144–145.

113 **"As much as I deplore violence"**: Ibid., 175.

114   **a disgrace to Jewish honor:** See Kamir, "Honor and Dignity
        Cultures."

114   **"Jews were to think big":** Ibid.

115   **"are required to denounce":** I owe much of this discussion to my
        former master's student Valerie Soon, now a PhD student at Duke
        University. In her final paper for my seminar, entitled "Honor,
        Dignity, and Collective Resistance," she argued that honor offers a
        more effective framework for battling oppression than dignity and
        invoked the writings of Stokely Carmichael and Charles Hamilton
        to go along with the arguments of Krause and Kamir.

115   **The nature of oppression makes it difficult:** Again, I'm grateful to
        Valerie Soon for these insights.

115   **he told me a good story:** Sommers, *Very Bad Wizard*, 105.

116   **controlling forces of the modern state:** See J. J. Brent and P. B.
        Kraska, "'Fighting Is the Most Real and Honest Thing': Violence
        and the Civilization/Barbarism Dialectic."

117   **"Fighting is the ticket":** Ibid., 365.

117   **"I've got school on Tuesday":** Ibid.

117   **"as a reflection of inner integrity":** Heith Copes et al.,
        "Peaceful Warriors: Codes for Violence Among Adult Male Bar
        Fighters," 763.

118   **"It's important to show who you are":** Ibid., 772.

118   **"That I just wasn't a man":** Ibid.

118   **"agro dudes that have something to prove":** Ibid., 773.

119   **"made reference to primitive man":** Ibid., 775.

119   **"will expand and trickle through":** Ibid.

120   **"Fighting also was perceived":** Ibid., 776.

120   **"if you're the person who starts it":** Ibid., 777.

120   **"I told him to back off":** Ibid., 774.

121   **"If you can already beat somebody up":** Ibid., 779.

122   **Fistfights were the ultimate sign:** Kennedy, *Don't Shoot*, 59.

122   **"I beat up some guy":** Copes et al., "Peaceful Warriors," 782.

123   **leads to greater cooperation:** Fieke Harinck et al., "The Good News About Honor Culture: The Preference for Cooperative Conflict Management in the Absence of Insults."

123   **"Conflicts might kill":** Christie, "Conflicts as Property," 1.

146   **they "dishonor the memory..."** http://blogs.timesofisrael.com /the-murder-of-innocents-and-evil-fruit/

CHAPTER FIVE

127   **"I look over to the girl":** Also from her essay: "The one thing that my dad didn't really teach me was the difference between a foul and not a foul. It was kind of a problem. Well not kind of."

130   **"sets an internal limit":** Robert Nozick, *Philosophical Explanations*, 366.

131   **"Revenge is personal":** Ibid., 367.

133   **"Tell me why he sacrificed her?":** Sophocles and Nicholas Rudall, *Electra*, 29.

133   **"Take a close look at yourself":** Ibid., 31.

134   **women in parts of southern Greece:** Blumenfeld, *Revenge*.

134   **"in which the corpse":** W. Miller, *Eye for an Eye*, 91.

135   **"Will you never learn to control":** Sophocles and Rudall, *Electra*, 20.

135   **"My whole life is spent seeking vengeance":** Ibid., 30.

136   **"Where is the freedom":** Ibid., 49.

138   **"No, I do not see":** Charles Portis, *True Grit*, 75.

138   **"I want him to know he is being punished":** Ibid., 97.

139   **"satisfaction not guaranteed" clause:** W. Miller, *Eye for an Eye*.

141   **"Forgetting was the way forward":** Blumenfeld, *Revenge*, 49.

142   **"you can't fuck with the Blumenfelds!":** Ibid., 114. I have a special fondness for this part of her story. I first discussed Blumenfeld's story in a presentation at the 2006 Society of Philosophy and Psychology meeting. It was one of my first major talks, a big success, and for the rest of the conference people would refer to me as the "Can't fuck with the Blumenfelds" guy.

142   **"It was about family":** Suzy Hansen, "Her Father's Keeper."

142 **"Anybody would do what my brother did":** Blumenfeld, *Revenge*, 6.

143 **"What if a Palestinian shoots a Jew?":** Ibid., 83.

144 **"I did it for one reason":** Ibid., 344.

145 **"Why did she use that word?":** Ibid., 348.

146 **"the shedding of innocent blood":** www.timesofisrael.com/liveblog _entry/rachelle-fraenkel-condemns-murder-of-abu-khdeir/.

CHAPTER SIX

155 **"The man is the source of life":** Aeschylus and Robert Fagles, *The Oresteia*, 260.

155 **"I honor the male in all things":** Ibid., 264.

156 **"Here in our homeland":** Ibid., 269.

159 **a "victims' rights" movement emerged:** See law.lclark.edu/centers/ national_crime_victim_law_institute/about_ncvli/history_of _victims_rights/ for more information on the victims rights movement.

160 **"personal responsibility and moral guilt":** *Booth v. Maryland*, 482 US 496 (1987), https://supreme.justia.com/cases/federal/us/482/ 496/case.html#515.

160 **"The focus of a VIS":** Ibid. (emphasis added).

160 **"can serve no other purpose":** Ibid.

161 **"rules of relevance that are older":** *Payne v. Tennessee*, 501 US 808 (1991), www.law.cornell.edu/supct/html/90–5721.ZD1.html.

162 **"Such testimony," the ruling stated:** *Robison v. Maynard*, 857 P.2d 817 (1992). law.justia.com/cases/oklahoma/court-of-appeals -civil/1992/15625.html.

162 **"nameless/faceless non-players":** law.lclark.edu/centers/national _crime_victim_law_institute/about_ncvli/history_of_victims _rights/.

163 **the upper and lower limits of deserved punishment:** Norval Morris, *Madness and the Criminal Law*.

164 **open to "a fundamental objection":** See Andrew Von Hirsch, "Proportionality and Desert, Reply to Bedau" and "Proportionality in the Philosophy of Punishment."

164 **Consider a recent trial:** I discuss this case and my objections to Von Hirsch in "Partial Desert" and "The Three Rs: Retribution, Revenge, and Reparation."

166 **crimes are not offenses against victims:** Recall Orit Kamir's remark about how dignity regards offenses and harms: "It shouldn't matter to us who the victim happened to be, through whom human dignity was abused, since it is the same dignity/value that we assign each and all of us, human beings."

167 **"The sentence imposed at the penalty stage":** *California v. Brown,* 479 US 538 (1987), http://caselaw.findlaw.com/us-supreme-court/479/538.html.

167 **"Right in its actuality":** Georg Hegel, *Philosophy of Right,* sec. 97a, as quoted in Igor Primoratz, *Justifying Legal Punishment.*

168 **credited with sparking the retributivist revival:** See Herbert Morris, "Persons and Punishment."

169 **why would they opt for a system:** The best defense of this theory is Primoratz, *Justifying Legal Punishment.*

171 **the way victims respond to insults and offenses:** See Dale T. Miller, "Disrespect and the Experience of Injustice."

172 **"so that the matter is resolved":** See Charles Barton's "Restorative Justice Empowerment," accessed at the Victim Offender Mediation Association website, www.voma.org/articles.shtml.

174 **"to change his position":** Christie, "Conflicts as Property," 2.

175 **a decrease in PTSD symptoms:** Mary P. Koss, "The RESTORE Program of Restorative Justice for Sex Crimes."

175 **"empowering rather than traumatizing":** Nadia M. Wager cited in Francesca Marsh and Nadia M. Wager, "Restorative Justice in Cases of Sexual Violence."

175 **In another recent study:** Ibid.

175 **"The victim is a particularly heavy loser"**: Christie, "Conflicts as Property," 8.

176 **These encounters help victims**: See, for example, Tinneke Van Camp and Jo-Anne Wemmers, "Victim Satisfaction with Restorative Justice."

177 **massive disproportional number of suspensions**: See, for example, Russell J. Skiba, Suzanne E. Eckes, and Kevin Brown, "African American Disproportionality in School Discipline: The Divide Between Best Evidence and Legal Remedy." See also the Advancement Project, "Test, Punish, and Push Out: How Zero Tolerance and High-Stakes Testing Funnel Youth into the School," www.advancementproject.org/resources/entry/test-punish-and -push-out-how-zero-tolerance-and-high-stakes-testing-funnel.

177 **"public schools into well-policed fortresses"**: Advancement Project, "Test, Punish, and Push Out."

177 **"In a truly victim-oriented system"**: Michael Moore, "Victims and Retribution: A Reply to Professor Fletcher," 77.

178 **in light of real cases**: Recall the trial in Grand Junction, Colorado, described earlier. In that case, the judge took the wishes of the victim into account, and it didn't seem unjust in the least.

178 **"reiterated his previous stance"**: John Braithwaite, "In Search of Restorative Jurisprudence," 347.

179 **"got neither his act of grace"**: Ibid.

179 **"At 2:15 in the afternoon"**: Paul Tullis, "Can Forgiveness Play a Role in Criminal Justice?," *New York Times*, January 5, 2013, www .nytimes.com/2013/01/06/magazine/can-forgiveness-play-a-role-in -criminal-justice.html.

CHAPTER SEVEN

188 **"unwritten rules of engagement"**: Bernstein, *The Code*, loc. 174, Kindle.

188 **"It's a living, breathing thing"**: Ibid., 805.

188 **"Spontaneous fights," writes Bernstein**: Ibid., 85.

188 **"Hockey is a game that polices itself":** Ibid., 60.

189 **"The basic premise of the code":** Ibid., 55.

189 **"It didn't matter if I didn't like":** Ibid., 116.

190 **Bruins-Canadiens "Brawl in the Hall":** You can see the famous brawl on YouTube: www.youtube.com/watch?v=FwRDsYrueUU.

190 **"Nowadays, players don't have to be accountable":** Bernstein, *The Code*, loc. 3190, Kindle.

191 **"and they relish the close bonds":** Ibid., 3405.

192 **"constantly reassuring each player":** Ibid., 3408.

192 **"a risk of having those situations":** Ibid., 3413.

192 **"to keep the peace":** Ibid., 3493.

193 **"It is a community where men will kill":** Kennedy, *Don't Shoot*, 20.

194 **"I didn't eat this morning":** From the excellent documentary *The Interrupters*, directed by Steve James, drawn originally from Alex Kotlowitz, "Blocking the Transmission of Violence," *New York Times Magazine*, May 4, 2008, www.nytimes.com/2008/05/04/magazine/04health-t.html.

195 **"Punishment doesn't drive behavior":** Kotlowitz, "Blocking the Transmission of Violence."

195 **"requires changing the social norms":** Jeffrey A. Butts et al., "Cure Violence: A Public Health Model to Reduce Gun Violence," 39.

195 **"The interrupters have to deal":** Kotlowitz, "Blocking the Transmission of Violence."

196 **"I felt like a punk":** Ibid.

196 **"Before Zale walked up to him":** Ibid.

197 **"must be slightly higher in status":** Mark Cooney, *Warriors and Peacemakers: How Third Parties Shape Violence*, 141.

197 **a second wave of surveys:** See Butts et al., "Cure Violence"; and Charles Ransford et al., "Report on the Cure Violence Model Adaptation in San Pedro Sula, Honduras."

198 **"Not an entire generation":** Kennedy, *Don't Shoot*, 43.

199 **"They do terrible things":** Ibid., 48.

200 **"Law enforcement, criminal justice"**: Ibid., 54.

201 **"We'll focus on everyone"**: Ibid., 65.

201 **GVI has met with great success**: See, for example, A. Braga and
     D. Weisburd, "The Effects of 'Pulling Levers' Focused Deterrence
     Strategies on Crime"; and the data at https://nnscommunities.org/
     our-work/strategy/group-violence-intervention.

201 **GVI's deal offers gangs and individuals**: Ibid., 71.

202 **"We had cops acting like social workers"**: Ibid., 73.

202 **"Aggression into Art"**: The phrase comes from Chang, *Can't Stop,
     Won't Stop*, quoting a *Village Voice* article on break-dancing battles
     in the 1970s.

203 **best insult for your opponent's mother**: The history of the dozens
     is fascinating itself, going back to the time of slavery. Until the late
     1970s, the dozens was confined mostly to street corners in black
     neighborhoods. It was a way for young black kids to exercise their
     minds—"like white people play Scrabble." One example:

> *I fucked your mama*
> *For a solid hour*
> *Baby came out*
> *Screaming Black Power.*
> (Elijah Wald, *The Dozens: A History of Rap's Mama*, 11)

204 **all races and cultural backgrounds**: The battle between
     Dumbfoundead (a Korean) and Tantrum (Chinese) (which you
     can see at www.youtube.com/watch?v=j0ZyNhsBWHc&t=1s) is
     one of the funniest battles I've ever seen. They spend their rounds
     trading Asian slurs. A sample from Tantrum's final round:

> *Even in here there's segregation*
> *I'm faster at solving test equations,*
> *basically I'm just a better Asian*

See I spit sicker and I rhyme fresher
I can kick quicker by a higher measure
And just to throw it in, my dick's bigger and I drive better!

204 **Loaded Lux condemns the destructive virtues"**: Shinga Mavima, "Bigger by the Dozens: The Prevalence of Afro-Based Tradition in Battle Rap," 86. Mavima offers an excellent account of battle rap's connection to the dozens and to the oral tradition of the griots in West Africa.

205 **the best battle round of all time:** You can watch the battle between Calicoe and Loaded Lux at www.youtube.com/watch?v=u1-z2hxXxKg&t=5s.

205 **"As Pharaoh Soul explained"**: Mavima, "Bigger by the Dozens," 100.

206 **"captured the liberal imagination"**: Chang, *Can't Stop, Won't Stop*, 156.

206 **a new Chicago program that in one year:** See www.youthguidance.org/bam/ and https://urbanlabs.uchicago.edu/projects/becoming-a-man for more details on the program and its results. See also Sara B. Heller et al., "Thinking, Fast and Slow? Some Field Experiments to Reduce Crime and Dropout in Chicago," on its results and an analysis of why it's successful.

207 **"The warrior who strikes his wife"**: Shannon E. French, *The Code of the Warrior: Exploring Warrior Values Past and Present*, 207.

208 **They learn a variety of practices and activities:** See Ulrich Boser, "The Youth-Counseling Program Helping to Curb Chicago's Violence."

208 **"For that matter, BAM never teaches"**: Heller et al., "Thinking, Fast and Slow?" (quote is from the working paper in 2015, 27).

208 **shift from moral rules to moral character:** The approach is also in line with Aristotelian and Stoic approaches toward building moral virtues, which emphasize practice and training over general moral principles. See the excellent work on this topic by Nancy Sherman such as *Stoic Warriors: The Ancient Philosophy Behind the Military*

Mind and *The Fabric of Character: Aristotle's Theory of Virtue* as well as my interview with her in *A Very Bad Wizard*.

209 **easier for members to develop strong social ties:** Again, see Boser, "Youth-Counseling Program." The strong social ties, Boser writes, "fosters a sense of belonging for BAM youth that influences positive identity development and, for some youth, extends to a broader sense of belonging with other prosocial networks."

209 **"a strong tendency to be moralistic":** Cooney, *Warriors and Peacemakers*, 141. See also Donald J. Black, *Social Structure of Right and Wrong*.

210 **turn their backs on mediation efforts:** Cooney, *Warriors and Peacemakers*; Black, *Social Structure of Right and Wrong*.

210 **"There was glory enough":** Kennedy, *Don't Shoot*, 235–236.

212 **"unfinished alternative" or a work in progress:** See Allegra McLeod, "Confronting Criminal Law's Violence: The Possibilities of Unfinished Alternatives."

EPILOGUE

217 **Human beings crave communal connections:** See, for example, Jonathan Haidt, *The Righteous Mind: Why Good People Are Divided by Politics and Religion*; and Haidt and Graham, "Planet of the Durkheimians." According to Haidt, moral values and intuitions are constructed from five basic foundations, and community/loyalty is one of them. Western liberals, informed by the morality of dignity, recognize only two of these foundations—harm/care and fairness—as legitimate. But they are in the vast minority of the world population. See also Alan Page Fiske's relationship-regulation theory in *Structures of Social Life: The Four Elementary Forms of Human Relations* and Fiske and Rai, *Virtuous Violence*. See also Henrich et al., "The Weirdest People in the World?," on the values of WEIRD cultures.

BIBLIOGRAPHY

Aeschylus and Robert Fagles. *The Oresteia.* New York: Penguin Books, 1979.

Aldous, Joan, et al. "An Exchange Between Durkheim and Tonnies on the Nature of Social Relations, with an Introduction by Joan Aldous." *American Journal of Sociology* 77, no. 6 (1972): 1191–1200. doi:10.1086/225264.

Anderson, Elijah. *Code of the Street: Decency, Violence, and the Moral Life of the Inner City.* New York: W. W. Norton, 2000.

Appiah, Anthony. *The Honor Code: How Moral Revolutions Happen.* New York: W. W. Norton, 2010.

Berger, Peter. "On the Obsolescence of the Concept of Honor." *European Journal of Sociology* 11, no. 2 (1970): 339–347.

Bernstein, Ross. *The Code: The Unwritten Rules of Fighting and Retaliation in the NHL.* Chicago: Triumph Books, 2006.

Black, Donald J. *Social Structure of Right and Wrong.* San Diego: Academic Press, 1993.

Black-Michaud, Jacob. *Cohesive Force: Feud in the Mediterranean and the Middle East.* Oxford: Blackwell, 1975.

Blumenfeld, Laura. *Revenge: A Story of Hope.* London: Picador, 2002.

Boehm, Christopher. *Blood Revenge: The Anthropology of Feuding in Montenegro and Other Tribal Societies.* Philadelphia: University of Pennsylvania Press, 1984.

Bonanno, Bill. *Bound by Honor: A Mafioso's Story.* New York: St. Martin's Paperbacks, 2000.

Boser, Ulrich. "The Youth-Counseling Program Helping to Curb Chicago's Violence." *Atlantic,* June 13, 2017. www.theatlantic.com/ education/archive/2017/06/inside-the-youth-counseling-program -helping-curb-chicagos-violence/529980/.

Bourdieu, Pierre. *Algeria, 1960: The Disenchantment of the World, The Sense of Honour, The Kabyle House or the World Reversed.* Translated by Richard Nice. Cambridge: Cambridge University Press, 1979.

Braga, A., and D. Weisburd. "The Effects of 'Pulling Levers' Focused Deterrence Strategies on Crime." *Campbell Systematic Reviews* 6 (April 2012): 1–91. doi:10.4073/csr.2012.6.

Braithwaite, John. *Crime, Shame and Reintegration.* Cambridge: Cambridge University Press, 1989.

———. "In Search of Restorative Jurisprudence." In *Restorative Justice and the Law,* edited by Lode Walgrave. London: Taylor and Francis, 2012.

Brent, J. J., and P. B. Kraska. "'Fighting Is the Most Real and Honest Thing': Violence and the Civilization/Barbarism Dialectic." *British Journal of Criminology* 53, no. 3 (2013): 357–377. doi:10.1093/bjc/azt001.

Brown, Ryan P. *Honor Bound: How a Cultural Ideal Has Shaped the American Psyche.* New York: Oxford University Press, 2016.

Busquet, Jacques. *Le droit de la vendetta et les paci corses.* Paris: A. Pedone, 1920.

Butts, Jeffrey A., et al. "Cure Violence: A Public Health Model to Reduce Gun Violence." *Annual Review of Public Health* 36, no. 1 (2015): 39–53. doi:10.1146/annurev-publhealth-031914–122509.

Campbell, J. K. "Honour and the Devil." In *Honour and Shame: The Values of Mediterranean Society,* edited by Jean G. Peristiany. Chicago: University of Chicago Press, 1966.

Carmichael, Stokely, and Charles V. Hamilton. *Black Power: The Politics of Liberation in America*. New York: Vintage Books, 1992.

Chang, Jeff. *Can't Stop, Won't Stop: A History of the Hip-Hop Generation*. New York: St. Martin's Press, 2005.

Christie, Nils. "Conflicts as Property." *British Journal of Criminology* 17, no. 1 (1977): 1–15. doi:10.1093/oxfordjournals.bjc.a046783.

Cohen, D., and J. A. Vandello. "The Paradox of Politeness." In *Cultural Shaping of Violence: Victimization, Escalation, Response*, edited by M. Anderson. West Lafayette, IN: Purdue University Press, 2004.

Cohen, Dov, et al. "Insult, Aggression, and the Southern Culture of Honor: An 'Experimental Ethnography.'" *Journal of Personality and Social Psychology* 70, no. 5 (1996): 945–960. doi:10.1037//0022-3514.70.5.945.

Collins, Randall. *Violence: A Micro-sociological Theory*. Princeton, NJ: Princeton University Press, 2009.

Cooney, Mark. *Warriors and Peacemakers: How Third Parties Shape Violence*. New York: New York University Press, 1998.

Copes, Heith, et al. "Peaceful Warriors: Codes for Violence Among Adult Male Bar Fighters." *Criminology* 51, no. 3 (2013): 761–794. doi:10.1111/1745-9125.12019.

Diamond, Jared. *The World Until Yesterday: What Can We Learn from Traditional Societies?* New York: Viking Penguin, 2012.

Douglass, Frederick. *Narrative of the Life of Frederick Douglass: An American Slave*. London: Chartwell Books, 2015.

Dubisch, Jill. *Gender & Power in Rural Greece*. Princeton, NJ: Princeton University Press, 1986.

Fiske, Alan Page. *Structures of Social Life: The Four Elementary Forms of Human Relations*. New York: Free Press, 1993.

Fiske, Alan Page, and Tage Shakti Rai. *Virtuous Violence: Hurting and Killing to Create, Sustain, End, and Honor Social Relationships*. Cambridge: Cambridge University Press, 2015.

French, Shannon E. *The Code of the Warrior: Exploring Warrior Values Past and Present*. Lanham, MD: Rowman and Littlefield, 2013.

Ginat, Joseph. *Blood Revenge: Family Honor, Mediation, and Outcasting*. Sussex: Sussex Academic Press, 2014.

Gregg, Gary S. *The Middle East: A Cultural Psychology*. Oxford: Oxford University Press, 2005.

Haidt, Jonathan. *The Righteous Mind: Why Good People Are Divided by Politics and Religion*. New York: Vintage Books, 2012.

Haidt, Jonathan, and Jesse Graham. "Planet of the Durkheimians, Where Community, Authority, and Sacredness Are Foundations of Morality." In *Social and Psychological Bases of Ideology and System Justification*, edited by J. Jost et al., 371–401. New York: Oxford University Press, 2009.

Haidt, Jonathan, and Selin Kesebir. "Morality." *Handbook of Social Psychology* (2010). doi:10.1002/9780470561119.socpsy002022.

Hansen, Suzy. "Her Father's Keeper." *Salon*, September 25, 2011. www.salon.com/2002/04/05/vengeance/.

Harinck, Fieke, et al. "The Good News About Honor Culture: The Preference for Cooperative Conflict Management in the Absence of Insults." *Negotiation and Conflict Management Research* 6, no. 2 (2013): 67–78. doi:10.1111/ncmr.12007.

Hasluck, Margaret. *Unwritten Law in Albania*. Cambridge: Cambridge University Press, 1954.

Hawdon, James, and John Ryan. "Social Relations That Generate and Sustain Solidarity After a Mass Tragedy." *Social Forces* 89, no. 4 (2011): 1363–1384. doi:10.1093/sf/89.4.1363.

———. "Social Solidarity Measure." *PsycTESTS Dataset* (2012). doi:10.1037/t28847–000.

Hawdon, James, et al. "Social Solidarity and Wellbeing After Critical Incidents: Three Cases of Mass Shootings." *Journal of Critical Incident Analysis* (2014): 1–24.

Heller, Sara B., et al. "Thinking, Fast and Slow? Some Field Experiments to Reduce Crime and Dropout in Chicago." *Quarterly Journal of Economics* (2016). doi:10.1093/qje/qjw033.

Henrich, Joseph, et al. *Foundations of Human Sociality: Economic Experiments and Ethnographic Evidence from Fifteen Small-Scale Societies.* Oxford: Oxford University Press, 2008.

———. "The Weirdest People in the World?" *Behavioral and Brain Sciences* 33, nos. 2–3 (2010): 61–83. doi:10.1017/s0140525x0999152x.

Henrich, Natalie, and Joseph Patrick Henrich. *Why Humans Cooperate: A Cultural and Evolutionary Explanation.* Oxford: Oxford University Press, 2007.

Jacquet, Jennifer. *Is Shame Necessary? New Uses for an Old Tool.* New York: Vintage Books, 2016.

Junger, Sebastian. *Tribe.* New York: Hachette, 2016.

Kadare, Ismail. *Broken April.* New York: New Amsterdam Books, 1989.

Kamir, Orit. "Applying Dignity, Respect, Honor and Human Rights to a Pluralistic, Multicultural Universe." Robert Schuman Centre for Advanced Studies research paper, July 2015. https://papers.ssrn.com/sol3/papers.cfm?abstract_id=2635489.

———. "Honor and Dignity Cultures: The Case of *Kavod* (Honor) and *Kvod Ha-adam* (Dignity) in Israeli Society and Law." In *The Concept of Human Dignity in Human Rights Discourse*, edited by David Kretzmer and Eckart Klein. The Hague: Kluwer Law International, 2002. www.global-report.com/common/attachment.php?d=kamir&a=3937.

Karon, Tony. "The Head Butt Furor: A Window on Europe's Identity Crisis." *Time*, July 13, 2006. content.time.com/time/world/article/0,8599,1213502,00.html.

Kennedy, David M. *Don't Shoot: One Man, a Street Fellowship, and the End of Violence in Inner-City America.* New York: Bloomsbury, 2011.

Koss, Mary P. "The RESTORE Program of Restorative Justice for Sex Crimes." *Journal of Interpersonal Violence* 29, no. 9 (2013): 1623–1660. doi:10.1177/0886260513511537.

Krause, Sharon R. *Liberalism with Honor.* Cambridge, MA: Harvard University Press, 2002.

Kretzmer, David, and Eckart Klein, eds. *The Concept of Human Dignity in Human Rights Discourse.* The Hague: Kluwer Law International, 2002.

Kundera, Milan. *The Unbearable Lightness of Being.* London: Faber and Faber, 1999.

Lancee, Bram, and Herman G. van de Werfhorst. "Income Inequality and Participation: A Comparison of 24 European Countries." *Social Science Research* 41, no. 5 (2012): 1166–1178. doi:10.1016/j .ssresearch.2012.04.005.

Leonard, Herman B., et al. "*Why* Was Boston Strong? Lessons from the Marathon Bombing." White paper, Harvard Kennedy School Program on Crisis Leadership, 2014. https://ash.harvard.edu/files/ why_was_boston_strong.pdf.

Luttrell, Marcus, and Patrick Robinson. *Lone Survivor: The Eyewitness Account of Operation Redwing and the Lost Heroes of SEAL Team 10.* New York: Little, Brown, 2007.

Maasdorp, James. "Zidane's Headbutt 10 Years On: The Hit That Shocked the Football World." *ABC News,* July 20, 2016. www.abc .net.au/news/2016–07–20/zinedine-zidane-headbutt-10-years-on -marco-materazzi/7645460.

Marsh, Francesca, and Nadia M. Wager. "Restorative Justice in Cases of Sexual Violence: Exploring the Views of the Public and Survivors." *Probation Journal* 62, no. 4 (2015): 336–356. doi:10.1177/0264550515619571.

Mavima, Shinga. "Bigger by the Dozens: The Prevalence of Afro-Based Tradition in Battle Rap." *Journal of Hip Hop Studies* 3, no. 1 (2016): 86–105.

McKay, Brett. Art of Manliness (blog), www.artofmanliness
.com/2012/10/01/manly-honor-part-i-what-is-honor/.

McLeod, Allegra. "Confronting Criminal Law's Violence: The Possibilities of Unfinished Alternatives." *Unbound* 8 (2012): 109–132.

Merriman, Ben. "Duels in the European Novel: Honor, Reputation, and the Limits of a Bourgeois Form." *Cultural Sociology* 9, no. 2 (2015): 203–219. doi:10.1177/1749975514561804.

Mill, John Stuart. *On Liberty*. London: John W. Parker and Son, 1859. www.gutenberg.org/files/34901/34901-h/34901-h.htm.

Miller, Dale T. "Disrespect and the Experience of Injustice." *Annual Review of Psychology* 52, no. 1 (2001): 527–553. doi:10.1146/annurev .psych.52.1.527.

Miller, William Ian. *Eye for an Eye*. Cambridge: Cambridge University Press, 2006.

———. *Humiliation, and Other Essays on Honor, Social Discomfort, and Violence*. Ithaca, NY: Cornell University Press, 1993.

Milloy, Courtland. "Gay Black Youths Go from Attacked to Attackers," *Washington Post*, September 27, 2011, www.washingtonpost.com/ local/gay-black-youths-go-from-attacked-to-attackers/2011/09/27/ gIQA2JV52K_story.html?utm_term=.c3c27e17f03a.

Moore, Michael. "Victims and Retribution: A Reply to Professor Fletcher." *Buffalo Criminal Law Review* 3, no. 1 (1999): 65–89. doi:10.1525/nclr.1999.3.1.65.

Morris, Herbert. "Persons and Punishment." *Monist* 52, no. 4 (1968): 475–501. doi:10.5840/monist196852436.

Morris, Norval. *Madness and the Criminal Law*. Chicago: University of Chicago Press, 1982.

National Crime Victim Law Institute. "History of Victims' Rights." 2011. law.lclark.edu/centers/national_crime_victim_law_institute/ about_ncvli/history_of_victims_rights/.

Nisbett, Richard E., and Dov Cohen. *Culture of Honor: The Psychology of Violence in the South*. Boulder, CO: Westview Press, 1996.

Nozick, Robert. *Philosophical Explanations*. Cambridge, MA: Harvard University Press, 1981.

Nye, Robert. "How the Duel of Honour Promoted Civility and Attenuated Violence in Western Europe." In *Honor, Violence, and Emotions in History*, edited by Carolyn Strange, Robert Cribb, and Christopher E. Forth. New York: Bloomsbury, 2014. Kindle.

Paskov, Marii, and Caroline Dewilde. "Income Inequality and Solidarity in Europe." *Research in Social Stratification and Mobility* 30, no. 4 (2012): 415–432. doi:10.1016/j.rssm.2012.06.002.

Pfaff, John F. *Locked In: The True Causes of Mass Incarceration—and How to Achieve Real Reform*. New York: Basic Books, 2017.

Pinker, Steven. *The Better Angels of Our Nature: A History of Violence and Humanity*. New York: Penguin Books, 2011.

Pitt-Rivers, J. A. (1965). Honour and Social Status. In J. G. Peristiany (ed.), *Honour and Shame: The Values of Mediterranean Society*. London: Weidenfeld and Norton.

Portis, Charles. *True Grit*. Woodstock, NY: Overlook Press, 2010.

Pressfield, Steven. *Gates of Fire: An Epic Novel of the Battle of Thermopylae*. New York: Bantam Books, 1998.

———. "The Warrior Ethos." February 9, 2011. www.stevenpressfield .com/category/the-warrior-ethos/.

Primoratz, Igor. *Justifying Legal Punishment*. Atlantic Highlands, NJ: Humanities Press, 1997.

Rai, Tage Shakti, and Alan Page Fiske. "Moral Psychology Is Relationship Regulation: Moral Motives for Unity, Hierarchy, Equality, and Proportionality." *Psychological Review* 118, no. 1 (2011): 57–75. doi:10.1037/a0021867.

Ransford, Charles, et al. "Report on the Cure Violence Model Adaptation in San Pedro Sula, Honduras." Cure Violence, 2016. http:// cureviolence.org/wp-content/uploads/2016/08/Report-on-the-Cure -Violence-Adaptation-in-San-Pedro-Sul.pdf.

Richerson, Peter J., and Robert Boyd. *Not by Genes Alone: How Culture Transformed Human Evolution.* Chicago: University of Chicago Press, 2005.

Sharp, Andrew. "The Miami Dolphins and Everything That Will Never Make Sense." *Grantland,* November 6, 2013. grantland.com/the-triangle/the-miami-dolphins-and-everything-that-will-never-make-sense/.

Shephard, Roy J., and Andris Rode. *The Health Consequences of "Modernization": Evidence from Circumpolar Peoples.* Cambridge: Cambridge University Press, 2008.

Sherman, Nancy. *The Fabric of Character: Aristotle's Theory of Virtue.* Oxford: Clarendon, 2004.

———. *Stoic Warriors: The Ancient Philosophy Behind the Military Mind.* New York: Oxford University Press, 2007.

Shryock, Andrew. "The New Jordanian Hospitality: House, Host, and Guest in the Culture of Public Display." *Comparative Studies in Society and History* 46, no. 1 (2004). doi:10.1017/s0010417504000039.

Skiba, Russell J., et al. "African American Disproportionality in School Discipline: The Divide Between Best Evidence and Legal Remedy." *New York Law Review* 54 (2009): 1071–1112.

Sommers, Tamler. "Partial Desert." In vol. 1 of *Oxford Studies in Agency and Responsibility,* edited by David Shoemaker, 246–262. Oxford: Oxford University Press, 2013.

———. *Relative Justice: Cultural Diversity, Free Will, and Moral Responsibility.* Princeton, NJ: Princeton University Press, 2012.

———. "The Three Rs: Retribution, Revenge, and Reparation." *Philosophia* 44, no. 2 (2016): 327–342. doi:10.1007/s11406–016–9706-y.

———. "The Two Faces of Revenge: Moral Responsibility and the Culture of Honor." *Biology & Philosophy* 24, no. 1 (2008): 35–50. doi:10.1007/s10539–008–9112–3.

———. *A Very Bad Wizard: Morality Behind the Curtain.* New York: Routledge, 2016.

Sophocles, and Nicholas Rudall. *Electra*. Chicago: Ivan R. Dee, 1993.

Stewart, Frank Henderson. *Honor*. Chicago: University of Chicago Press, 1994.

Strange, Carolyn, et al., eds. *Honour, Violence and Emotions in History*. New York: Bloomsbury, 2014.

"Test, Punish and Push Out: How Zero Tolerance and High-Stakes Testing Funnel Youth into the School." Advancement Project, 2010. www.advancementproject.org/resources/entry/test-punish-and -push-out-how-zero-tolerance-and-high-stakes-testing-funnel.

Turbow, Jason, and Michael Duca. *The Baseball Codes: Beanballs, Sign Stealing, and Bench-Clearing Brawls—the Unwritten Rules of America's Pastime*. New York: Anchor Books, 2010.

Van Boekel, Martin, et al. "Effects of Participation in School Sports on Academic and Social Functioning." *Journal of Applied Developmental Psychology* 46 (2016): 31–40. doi:10.1016/j.appdev.2016.05.002.

Van Camp, Tinneke, and Jo-Anne Wemmers. "Victim Satisfaction with Restorative Justice." *International Review of Victimology* 19, no. 2 (2013): 117–143. doi:10.1177/0269758012472764.

Vandello, Joseph A., et al. "U.S. Southern and Northern Differences in Perceptions of Norms About Aggression." *Journal of Cross-Cultural Psychology* 39, no. 2 (2008): 162–177. doi:10.1177/0022022107313862.

Von Hirsch, Andrew. "Proportionality and Desert, Reply to Bedau." *Journal of Philosophy* 75, no. 11 (1978): 622–624. doi:10.5840/jphil197875116.

———. "Proportionality in the Philosophy of Punishment." *Crime and Justice* 16 (1992): 55–98. doi:10.1086/449204.

Wald, Elijah. *The Dozens: A History of Rap's Mama*. New York: Oxford University Press, 2012.

INDEX

JAIME LAGDAMEO

Tamler Sommers is associate professor of philosophy at the University of Houston. He is the author of two previous books, *Relative Justice: Cultural Diversity, Free Will, and Moral Responsibility* (Princeton, 2012) and *A Very Bad Wizard: Morality Behind the Curtain* (Routledge, 2016), and cohost of the *Very Bad Wizards* podcast. He lives in Houston, Texas, with his wife and daughter and two dogs of uncertain breed.